I Golfed Across

MONGOLIA

I Golfed Across

MONGOLIA

HOW AN IMPROBABLE ADVENTURE HELPED ME
REDISCOVER THE SPIRIT OF GOLF (AND LIFE)

Andre Tolme

THUNDER'S MOUTH PRESS
NEW YORK

I GOLFED ACROSS MONGOLIA:
HOW AN IMPROBABLE ADVENTURE HELPED ME REDISCOVER THE
SPIRIT OF GOLF (AND LIFE)

Published by
Thunder's Mouth Press
An Imprint of Avalon Publishing Group, Inc.
245 West 17th Street, 11th floor
New York, NY 10011

AVALON
publishing group incorporated

Library of Congress Cataloging-in-Publication Data is available.

ISBN-13: 978-1-56025-822-3
ISBN-10: 1-56025-822-5

9 8 7 6 5 4 3 2 1

Book design by Maria E. Torres

Printed in the United States of America
Distributed by Publishers Group West

André golfs past a group of gers. *Photo credit: André Tolmé*

A televised archery competition at the Naadam Festival. *Photo credit: David Tolmé*

Right: The "pull-cart" used on holes four through six. *Photo credit: André Tolmé*

Grazing horses and sheep. *Photo credit: David Tolmé*

Russian motorcycles, like this one with a sidecar, complement the more traditional method of transportation—the horse. *Photo credit: André Tolmé*

Locals in Dornod Province try out the game of golf for the first time. *Photo credit: André Tolmé*

A thumbs-up sign and a smile means all is well for this rural family. *Photo credit: André Tolmé*

Right: Boldoo and Bataa. Two of the three brothers who helped revive my will to continue. *Photo credit: André Tolmé*

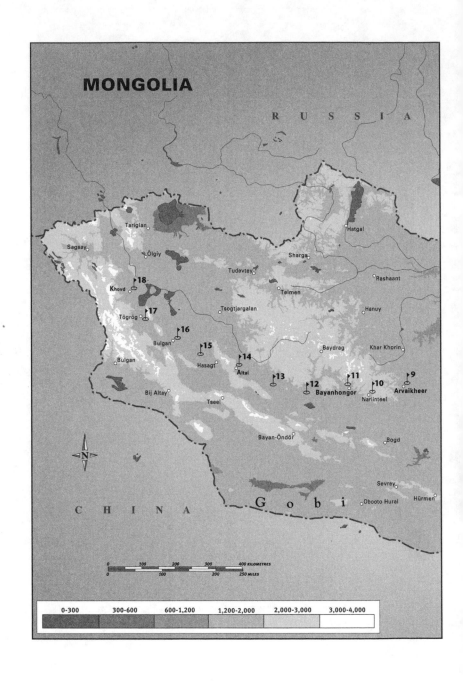

MONGOLIA

R U S S I A

Tariglan
Hatgal
Sagsay
Ölgiy
Sharga
Tudevtey
Rashaant
Khovd ⊳18
Telmen
Tögrög ⊳17
Tsogtjargalan
Hanuy
⊳16
Bulgan ⊳15
Baydrag
Khar Khorin
Bulgan
Hasagt ⊳14
Altai
⊳13
⊳12 ⊳11 ⊳10 ⊳9
Bij Altay
Bayanhongor Arvaikheer
Tseel
Nariinteel

Bayan-Öndör
Bogd

N

Sevrey
C H I N A
G o b i
Obooto Hural Hürmen

| 0 | 100 | 200 | 300 | 400 KILOMETRES |
| 0 | 100 | 200 | 250 MILES |

| 0-300 | 300-600 | 600-1,200 | 1,200-2,000 | 2,000-3,000 | 3,000-4,000 |

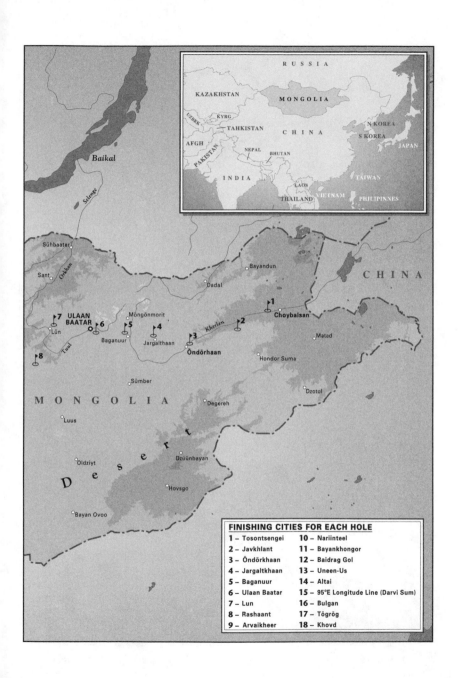

FINISHING CITIES FOR EACH HOLE

1 – Tosontsengei	**10** – Nariinteel
2 – Javkhlant	**11** – Bayankhongor
3 – Öndörkhaan	**12** – Baidrag Gol
4 – Jargaltkhaan	**13** – Uneen-Us
5 – Baganuur	**14** – Altai
6 – Ulaan Baatar	**15** – 95°E Longitude Line (Darvi Sum)
7 – Lun	**16** – Bulgan
8 – Rashaant	**17** – Tögrög
9 – Arvaikheer	**18** – Khovd

The second shot of the expedition, near Choybalsan. *Photo credit: Alain Vandenplas*

The first caddy of the expedition, Sogoo, and his UAZ jeep. *Photo credit: André Tolmé*

T he tent is rolling end over end, its self-supporting frame keeping its shape as it bounces on the short grass. Even if you've never seen a nylon dome-shaped tent tumbling in circles in the wind on the open prairie, the image comes easily to mind. It's an image of disaster. Like an unattended baby carriage rolling down a hill in the middle of traffic, something has gone horribly wrong. This particular tent is a light blue Sierra Designs Orion AST, a lightweight backpacking tent that can sleep two, although one person fits much more comfortably. And this particular tent has about a five-meter head start on me.

I'm reminded of what Henry Miller once wrote: "There's nothing more ridiculous than a man chasing his hat down the street in the wind." He's right. A pathetic, pitiful man reaching down to grasp his fedora, while the wind gusts at just the right moment to screw him over again and again, is indeed ridiculous. People are funny that way—laughing at the misfortune of others. It's a little sick, but it seems like we can't help ourselves. And if there was a camera crew in a helicopter floating high above the Mongolian steppe on this particular morning recording me as I sprint after my tent, well, that would be fucking hilarious.

For me, however, this is deadly serious, because my tent is not just cartwheeling aimlessly across the steppe, just beyond the reach of my outstretched arms; it's rolling directly toward the Kherlen River. It took less than a second for my body to lurch into a full sprint when my tent made its first revolution in that gust of wind from the north, but that delay in reaction time was enough for the tent to gain its five-meter advantage. I'm barefoot as I run, but my feet barely feel the sharp pebbles and thorny weeds. I'm focused on the tent, and adrenaline has taken over. My physical reaction was quick, but mentally it's taken a few seconds for the picture to become clear: "If I don't catch that tent in the next ten seconds, it's going into the river." Concern has given way to panic.

The Kherlen River flows east, meandering down from the Khentii mountain range in north central Mongolia to the large stagnant Hulun Lake, just across the border in China. The river cuts deeply into the flat, dry landscape of the steppe, picking up sand and silt as it erodes the river banks. The muddy brown water flows rapidly, with churning eddies and foaming ripples of white water breaking the surface. At this bend of the river where I had just slept the previous night, the water level is far enough below the riverbank that I can't see the surface as I sprint toward it. But I can hear it, gurgling and growling like a hungry bear, and the panic grows. It's as if the wind and the water have conspired to play a most horrible trick on me. Helplessness and panic vie for control of my mind as I watch in horror as my tent takes one last bounce up into the air before disappearing over the edge of the bank. I'm still running at full speed as I approach the bank myself, and the thought becomes clear in my mind: "I may die jumping into that river, but without my tent I'm surely dead." I have a decision to make.

Sprinting barefoot while chasing a tent across a vast, empty landscape without another person around for miles is not something I'd ever imagined doing. As the rushing water comes into view, I wonder in the most general way: "What the hell *am* I doing?" Here's the short answer: I am golfing across Mongolia. I am attempting to achieve what no one else has most likely even contemplated before—to whack a little white ball across the natural terrain of an entire country that's almost the size of California, Arizona, New Mexico, and Texas combined. It's an unusual quest, I admit. But for me, it doesn't seem so odd. In fact, my life has been very unordinary lately, and it all began two and a half years ago.

"I'm going to quit and travel around the world for a year." These were perhaps the most decisive words I've ever uttered, and the first in a series of decisions that have put me in my current predicament. I spoke these words in December 2000 to John, my boss in the construction services division of an international environmental engineering firm. John is a short, stocky man with a full beard and is perhaps the best supervisor that one could hope for. He has the ability to reprimand and compliment at the same time, to encourage his employees to do their best work by offering to work just as hard himself to help. John knows the engineering profession well, but he also knows that employees are people with their own lives, and perhaps this is why I'm so emotional when I tell him of my plans. I'd been at the firm for four years and had developed a promising career as an engineer at one of the largest and most respected engineering companies in the world. A few months earlier, John had called me and told me that he had gotten me a raise in pay, even though it was September and raises are typically given at the end of the year.

I was a young single man living in the San Francisco Bay Area, arguably one of the best places to live in the world. I had a company truck to drive to the job site every day and my own Jeep Wrangler to drive around with on weekends in the perennial California sunshine. My 401(k) retirement plan was growing. I played golf nearly every weekend. I had lots of great friends. And I was about to give it all up.

It took all the courage I could summon just to ask John if he could spare a minute to speak with me. He closed the door to my office in the portable construction site trailer, and with his typical concerned voice asked, "What's up?" I was frightened and numb. I felt as if I no longer had control of my body. It had taken all my strength just to get to this moment, and as I told John of my plans, I feared that I was making the biggest mistake of my life. I'm not an overly emotional man, but at that moment, tears began to well in my eyes from the agony of making such an enormous decision. From this point forward, I would throw away all of the stability and security I had built in my life and march forward into unknown territory. I felt as if I were about to jump into a raging river. Now, a couple of years later, I am about to do exactly that.

While the real possibility existed that I could drown in the river trying to rescue my tent, it was a bit of an exaggeration to think that I'd die if I let it float away. I could always find my way back to the main road, hitchhike back to Ulaan Baatar, Mongolia's capital city, and stay in a cozy guest house while I figured out what to do next. But that would probably mean that I'd have to leave Mongolia and fly to some country where they sold high-quality tents, and then return as quickly as possible to where I had left off. This would not only be expensive but also very time-consuming, and would probably mean that I wouldn't be able to accomplish my goal of golfing across Mongolia this year.

Planning and performing this expedition had been the focus of my life for the past six months. I had persuaded sponsors to put their trust in me and contribute financially to my unique project. I had sent out a press release. *Outside* magazine was already working on a story about me for their upcoming issue, and my hometown newspaper had written a glowing article about the local kid with big ideas. The possibility of failure, and especially failure due to something as stupid as removing my tent stakes without securing my tent first, was incomprehensible to me, and therefore I equated it with death. Like I said, it was a bit of an exaggeration, but perhaps that's what I needed to tell myself so I could work up enough courage to take a running leap into the Kherlen River. So I jumped. It was a jump into the dark unknown, but it wasn't my first one. Two and a half years earlier, I had also leaped into the unknown when I made the decision to quit my job and leave behind the cozy life I had built.

John had arranged a leave of absence with the corporate human resources department so that I could return to my job in December 2001. This made me feel a little more comfortable as I boarded a bus to Mexico with a tidy one-year travel itinerary planned. My travels would take me to five continents, ending with a return flight to California. It was a reassuring thought to know that I could have everything back in exactly twelve months, as if nothing had ever happened. What I didn't realize at the time, though, was how much I would change in that year. When the one-year deadline had passed, I was in Kathmandu, Nepal, planning a ten-day whitewater rafting trip down the Karnali River. John had sent me an e-mail asking if he should start thinking about projects for me to work on. I'm sure he knew the answer before I replied. There was no way that I was ready to go back to an ordinary life. I had seen otherworldly landscapes on the high desert plains of Bolivia. I had spent days chatting with monks and drinking yak-butter tea in Tibet. I was about to run a river from the Himalayan mountains to the jungles of the Indian subcontinent. I was floating along blissfully in my travels, negotiating the troubled waters of foreign cultures and riding the currents of adventure, and I was having the time of my life. My decision to give up a comfortable life for one of exploration and uncertainty was the best decision I had ever made.

My travels took me from the jungles of South America to the Arctic Circle in northern Scandinavia, and to remote and seldom-visited countries such as Mongolia. And it was in this little-known land between Russia and China where an incredible inspiration struck me.

I had met some fascinating people in my travels, including a Frenchman in Brazil who was cycling around the world. On a previous adventure, he had spent a year and a half jogging around every country in Europe. Now, he was undertaking an even grander adventure that would take up to twenty years and have him pedaling his bicycle on every continent. He told me about other adventurers who had stopped at nothing to pursue their dreams including two men who had sailed an upside-down Volkswagen Beetle across the Atlantic, and a Japanese man who had pushed a shopping cart while jogging from Asia to Europe. I met an Austrian man in Peru who was planning on walking across the entire Amazon jungle from west to east. These men had something in common; most people would call them crazy, but in fact they were absolutely sane, perfectly normal. They were inspired and focused to achieve the adventure of their lifetimes; and, hearing their stories, I began to develop a longing for a focused and inspired adventure of my own.

I had only planned to spend a few days in Mongolia, a brief stop between more lengthy travels in Russia and China. However, I quickly learned that if I only visited Mongolia's largest city and capital, Ulaan Baatar, then I'd miss out on the real beauty of a unique land. It would be like visiting Kenya and opting to stay in Nairobi without a safari adventure on the savannah. Mongolia's charms are found not in its cities but in the undeveloped reaches of the countryside, where semi-nomadic herders have lived much the same way for thousands of years. Mongolians live from the meat and milk of their animals and inhabit round, white tents called *gers,* also known as yurts to many Westerners. A visit to Mongolia's countryside is like traveling back in time, and the nation remains one of the last great adventure destinations in Asia.

I teamed up with Bas, Daniel, and Natasha, my new friends who I had met at various stages in my travels, and we hired a Mongolian driver with an old Russian four-wheel-drive van for a tour across Mongolia's open steppe. These were the grasslands where Genghis Khan had begun his empire which stretched across Asia into Europe, and where I learned that travel by horse was in many ways more comfortable than travel by auto. Mongolia's highways are potholed dirt tracks that bounce and weave their way across the open landscape, and travel on them is a dusty, bone-jarring experience. Sleeping in Mongolian homes every night, we were completely immersed in the local culture. We rode horses and camels in the day and sampled fermented horse milk, dried curd, and the dreadfully potent Mongolian vodka at night. The dried curd could be sour or rancid-tasting, but was always hard as a rock. The horse milk was a pungent, acrid concoction of sour milk with tiny alcoholic bubbles, and the local vodka could be better put to use cleaning a carburetor. The food was awful, but we were always offered plenty of it. One consistent trait of Mongolians is their generous hospitality. Enormous bowls of milk or curd were always being proffered in our direction, and once a vodka bottle is opened, it is always finished. Without a doubt, it was the unlimited generosity of the people that made me realize that this was a special place and, to a degree I couldn't fully understand at the time, made me feel as if I were at home.

I'm not sure whether it was the vodka or the fizzy horse-milk alcohol, but, standing alone outside a ger one evening and gazing off toward the horizon as the sun set on the treeless plains, I thought of golf. "This country is one giant golf course!" I thought. My favorite weekend pastime had been missing from my life during my journey around the world, and I began to crave the feeling of connecting with a solid driver off the tee, watching the ball leap off the sweet spot of the club and fly magically ahead over the fairway. As I stared off toward the distance, the short grass and rolling terrain transformed itself from Mongolia's predominant geographical feature—the steppe—to that of something more familiar to me, an enormous fairway. I thought it might be possible to hit a golf ball in this natural terrain, and in fact that it might be possible to hit it all day long. And then the ultimate thought came to me: "I wonder if it's possible to hit a golf ball across the entire country."

At the time, I had no idea that a year later, I'd be at the start of the grandest adventure of my life, or that I'd find myself swimming the turbulent waters of the Kherlen River on a rescue mission for a tent. But here I am now, in midair, with an immediate goal in mind. Like all of the decisions that led me to this point in time, it's too late to change my mind.

I'm relieved when my feet don't feel the bone-wrecking smack of a boulder or the flesh-ripping jab of a tree limb but instead plunge into the deep water with a soft landing. The muddy water roils around me, and I manage to get my head above the surface as I open my eyes to gain sight of my tent. Miraculously, it still sits on the water's surface only an arm's length away from me. The current sweeps us both downstream, but with a few furious paddles I manage to reach the tent before it fills with water and sinks into the depths forever. I tread water with one hand while the other grasps a fistful of nylon fabric wrapped around a slim aluminum pole. I struggle through the current, kicking with both feet and paddling with my left arm, while I hold my prize high in the air with my right hand. I reach the soft mud of the river's shore only fifty meters downstream from where I jumped in, and I exhale the breath that I've probably been holding throughout the ordeal. I'm alive and my tent is still intact and firmly in my possession. The adrenaline still fills my veins, and my heart is beating quickly as I laboriously climb the loose riverbank and walk back across the grassy terrain toward the remaining items of my camp.

Methodically, I dismantle the tent and pack it away, and then I strip off my wet clothes to hang around the outside of my backpack. Only after I've changed into my only spare set of dry clothes does the seriousness of the situation fade a bit and I permit myself an amused laugh accompanied by an honest smile. "That was pretty stupid." Stupid? Idiotic is more like it. I chuckle again as an earlier thought comes back to me. "What the hell am I doing?" This thought will haunt me repeatedly over the next several weeks.

This is day two of the Golf Mongolia Expedition. Yesterday, I started golfing from the city of Choibalsan with my final destination more than thirteen hundred miles away. I was filled with optimism and confidence, and I golfed nearly seven miles with seventy-two swings of my three-iron. Today, the sun has just risen but I'm already cold, wet, and humbled. I've made a mistake that almost ended the entire expedition before it really began. I'm sure it won't be my last mistake, but I'm glad that I somehow managed to get myself out of this bad situation. I'll need all the self-confidence I can generate during this bizarre adventure, because I'm doing it alone, and, more important, no one has ever done anything like it before.

I'm walking through the cavernous departure hall of the Beijing Central Railway Station the way a chimpanzee would walk through a crowded shopping mall. I'm completely lost, but I can't help but have a look around. I've just made it through a swarming line of people in the entrance to the station, where I had to stand in front of a thermal imaging machine that probably bombarded my brain with radiation. I think it was meant to check whether I had a fever, though it would be hard to tell with the mass of humanity and body heat surrounding me. Despite the aggressive actions of other travelers struggling to be the next victim to stand on the little foot-shaped outlines painted on the floor and get their heads checked, the screening procedure is well organized. Dozens of police officers and station agents wearing masks over their mouths methodically herd us through the remote fever detector, and then a metal detector, into the free-for-all area of the central lobby. A voice from above announces train arrivals and departures in Chinese over a scratchy PA system that echoes off the lobby walls. Or at least that's what I think the voice is saying; I can't understand a thing. Maybe they're telling everyone to evacuate the building immediately. Maybe they're announcing the lunch specials in the station restaurant. The way that the Chinese people all around me are scampering back and forth, either option is plausible. I'm absolutely clueless, so I just walk straight ahead.

Through some miracle of divine intervention, or perhaps chimpanzee intuition, I come to the end of the hall and stare at a sign that says, in English, "International Train Waiting Hall." This looks like exactly where I'm supposed to be. But first I've got to get past another checkpoint, protected by another group of mask-wearing officers. One of them hands me a sheet of paper.

Please indicate if you have any of the following symptoms:

Fever _____

Vomiting _____

Headache _____

Diarrhea _____

It's May 2003, and this is a SARS medical evaluation checklist. For the past six months, the Severe Acute Respiratory Syndrome outbreak has had daily coverage in the world media. And even though the hysteria of a possible international pandemic has waned in the last few weeks, the Chinese are still taking the issue seriously. Most of the reported cases and casualties from the nearly incurable virus have come from China. And China, as it happens, is the first destination in Asia for the Golf Mongolia Expedition. Three days ago, I departed Los Angeles with a backpack full of camping gear, a large box of golf balls, two golf clubs (a three-iron and a backup four-iron), and a full supply of optimism. My stopover in Beijing lasted three days, and now I'm taking the final steps toward Mongolia. If only I can make it to the train.

Peering at the medical checklist, I'm silently wondering what kind of an idiot would voluntarily answer yes to any of these questions. Even if I did have any of these symptoms, the last thing I'd want to do is raise any eyebrows and get whisked away to a Chinese hospital full of people who actually do have SARS.

Although, if I were being completely honest, I'd have to place a check mark next to the word *diarrhea*. General Tso's chicken, or perhaps some of his military comrades, have been waging a small war in my intestines since I arrived in China. Diarrhea is a fairly common experience for newly arrived foreigners in this country. And seeing the word *headache* on the checklist is a not-too-subtle reminder that I should have passed on the Chinese Mao Tai whiskey last night. Mao Tai is China's best-known indigenous liquor, although "whiskey" is much too generous a euphemism for the potent concoction that smells like kerosene strained though rotten vegetables. I believe it's actually made from fermented sorghum, although I'm not positive about this and, for that matter, I'm not even sure what sorghum is.

But I've got a ticket for the Beijing–Ulaan Baatar train and I don't want to delay this journey to the country where I'll spend the next four months hitting golf balls. I sneak a furtive glance up at the young man dressed in a green police uniform. He's stone-faced and probably doesn't sense my nervousness. I sign the paper and place it in his white-gloved hands and he nonchalantly tosses it onto a large pile of similar papers and ushers me through a door into another waiting hall. I feel like I've passed an enormous test.

The next hall is also packed with people. Most are crowded around the doors, waiting for the station agents to grant them access to the platform. Everyone wants to get on the train quickly along with their bags, boxes, and crates of goods that they're taking to Mongolia. This is theoretically a passenger train, but it'll be stuffed with commercial goods—clothes, kitchen utensils, and foods—which Mongolians hope to sell for a profit in the markets of Ulaan Baatar.

The shoulder strap of my duffel bag digs into my skin as I lug it and my two backpacks over to a corner of the hall. It's no surprise: there are nearly five hundred golf balls inside, and it weighs at least fifty pounds. The bag is a North Face counterfeit that I bought in a

Beijing market yesterday for fifty yuan ($6), and the zipper is already broken after one day of use. That's the problem I've noticed with buying cheap imitation clothing and luggage in Asian markets—crappy zippers. Zipper quality is always the easiest way to tell the shoddy imitation goods from the authentic ones, and it's the number one complaint of knockoff clothing buyers. I knew this very well when I haggled for the bag, but I still didn't expect it to break after only one day.

The bag is the least important of three purchases I made while stopping over in Beijing on my way to Mongolia: it only needs to last until I reach Ulaan Baatar, while my new water bottle and cooking pots will need to last the entire journey. I spent nearly a thousand dollars purchasing equipment for this trip in an outdoor equipment store in California. New boots, GPS receiver, multifuel stove, etc. It added up fast; and when I realized that I probably didn't have enough money in my bank account to pay the credit card bill, I got squeamish. "I'll buy the last few things in China," I told myself. So here I am now, putting my faith in something called a Yingxing cup. As far as I can tell, it's exactly the same as a Nalgene water bottle, the clear plastic container that every hiker or granola-eating, vegan, health-conscious environmentalist wannabe keeps dangling from his or her backpack. I just couldn't bring myself to pay ten dollars for a piece of plastic, so now I've got a one-dollar piece of plastic.

I may have actually lucked out on this one. After I brought my new Yingxing cup, I was pleasantly surprised to find that it screws onto the bottom of my water filter exactly as its name-brand competitor does. I've never been one to express much brand loyalty before, but I have a new fondness for the Yingxing brand. And there are no zippers to worry about. I'm equally optimistic about the set of stainless-steel cooking pots I paid two dollars for. The brand name is written all in Chinese characters, but I'm sure it must say something like "Super Star Quality Brand."

I have no choice but to be optimistic. This is the boldest, craziest, most unprepared thing I've ever done, and it's too late to turn back. I've always thought that making the decision to stand in line for the roller coaster is more difficult than actually riding it. Once the crowd starts to push you along, your fate has been determined and it's futile to resist: pray for strength and enjoy the ride. My ride has yet to begin, but getting on the train to Mongolia will bring me one step closer, and now the guards are opening the doors. Within seconds, the volume rises and the waiting room becomes a frenzy of human bodies pushing and struggling through the two sets of double doors, so I patiently wait in the corner for the commotion to diminish before slinging the half-zipped duffel bag and other luggage up onto my shoulders. Once the cacophony and frenetic action die down, I glance at my ticket to check the car and seat numbers and make my way out onto the platform.

I'm pleasantly surprised when I locate my cabin and find it

empty. It's a four-berth sleeper cabin that wears the grime of thousands of journeys between China, Mongolia, and Russia, but it'll be my home for the next thirty hours. I lift my bags up into the overhead space that extends out over the hallway, and I'm soon joined by Lena and Wiebke, and then by Sam. Lena and Wiebke are German graphic-design students who had been studying in China; Sam is an Australian tour guide who is on his way to Mongolia for four months of shepherding tourists around the vast Mongolian countryside. Sam and I exchange a knowing look that conveys a simple message—"Aren't we lucky bastards to be sharing this berth with two attractive young women." It's a silly thought, really, but seems to function as an immediate form of male bonding. Most men feel somehow special or fortunate when they're seated next to an attractive female, as if they've won some cosmic lottery or something.

"What's your story?" Sam shoots at me in that typically friendly, matter-of-fact, "isn't life a big party and I don't know why you Yanks and Pommies take it so seriously and I'd much rather be drinking a beer" Australian fashion. I return his smirking expression and, knowing the Australians' love of sarcasm, I pronounce with a straight face: "I'm going to become the first person to golf across Mongolia." After a brief moment of silence, I call my own bluff and hand the three of them my business card which does in fact proclaim that I am "one man hitting a golf ball across Mongolia."

"Is this for real?" they all inquire simultaneously.

"Two thousand kilometers. It should take me about four months," I reply.

"This is awesome! Are you sponsored by anyone?"

I don't let on that this is a sore spot for me. I had spent the previous three months cold-calling all the major golf companies and many outdoor gear suppliers, without much success. This failure to land a major sponsor nagged at me despite the fact that I had worked hard in the planning and preparation of the expedition, and it was now progressing according to plan. It bugged me so much because I felt that having corporate backing would have somehow given the expedition greater legitimacy. And it also engendered a sense of outrage that every person I met and told of my plan thought it was the coolest thing they'd heard in ages, while all the golf companies politely told me "We're not interested." I felt indignant that they didn't sponsor me. It was unjust.

"I got a free tent and I have a lot of small individual sponsors," I answer meekly. This is true, although I don't bother to mention that the small, individual sponsors are mostly family members or close friends.

"Are you using orange golf balls?" asks Lena. I can tell that she doesn't know a thing about golf and is quite proud of her question.

"No, I'm a traditional golfer," I reply. "Real golfers only use white balls. Orange balls are tacky." I like the embedded irony of stating that I'm a traditional golfer, while in the same sentence mentioning that I'm the first person to ever embark on a long-distance extreme golf expedition.

I pull a map of Mongolia out of my backpack and spread it out on the tiny table in front of the window. "Here's where I'm starting," I announce, pointing my finger at a city in eastern Mongolia named Choibalsan. "The north of Mongolia borders Siberia and is mostly forests. The south is mostly the Gobi Desert. Across the middle," I say, sliding my index finger in a broad sweep across the length of the map, "is where the good golf is. This is the steppe." We all gaze at the map silently for a moment, examining Mongolia's borders and other geographic features. "I'm going to finish there, in Khovd," I say, pointing to a city on the opposite end of the map. Looking at the full view of the map again, I'm impressed with how big Mongolia is. More than fifteen hundred miles from end to end. "Wow, that's a long way," Lena points out. "That's exactly what I was thinking," I respond, laughing.

The train jerks backward and then forward before slowly gaining speed as it pulls out of the station. The conversation moves away from golf to the topic du jour—SARS. My companions had all had their plans altered because of the outbreak. The two women had cut short their stay at a university in northern China, because they were essentially quarantined prisoners on the campus who were only allowed to venture out into the unremarkable city when supervised by a representative of the school. Sam had been drinking beer and flirting with the local girls in a small city in Yunnan Province for the past few weeks because almost all of his tours had been cancelled. Without doubt, the SARS outbreak was serious business. Hundreds of people had died from the virus, and many health officials believed a worldwide epidemic was possible. It wouldn't have been the first deadly epidemic to have originated in Asia.

The bubonic plague, otherwise known as the Black Death, killed a quarter of the population of Europe in the thirteenth century, and it also had its origins in Asia. Many historians attribute the spread of the disease to the Mongolians, who carried it with them as they conquered Central Asia and pushed into Eastern Europe. Some even claim that the fierce Mongolian warriors, while besieging cities near the Caspian Sea, catapulted infected corpses over the city walls as a form of biological warfare. I doubt this story is true, but I never miss a chance to retell it. I love the imagery of Mongolian marauders laughing while dead bodies spin through the air and plop down in the town square as women and children run screaming. It has Hollywood written all over it.

No one is certain exactly how the Black Death reached Europe, and some scientists are now disputing that it was a form of bubonic plague at all. One thing is certain, though: bubonic plague still exists, and one place where it is common is Mongolia. I had been shocked to learn this during my first visit to Mongolia. Bubonic plague is something that you learn about in history class, not a disease that you should worry about contracting. Yet every year, hundreds of people die from bubonic plague, and there are frequent outbreaks in the

Mongolian countryside. Most cases come from people eating infected marmot meat. Marmots are prairie dog–like animals that flourish in the grasslands of central Asia, and they apparently taste quite scrumptious. I've got some antibiotics with me that I could take in case I notice my flesh starting to turn black after eating some Mongolian mystery meat, but I'm hoping to avoid contact with the rodents altogether.

Our train compartment gets a little more crowded when Alain, a thirty-something Belgian traveler, joins us. He had had the misfortune of being placed in a cabin with three Mongolians and their dozens of boxes that filled every available inch of space, including Alain's seat. As the train rocks steadily down the tracks, I repeat my story to Alain, who hits me with some tough questions.

"How many golf balls are you taking with you?"

"About five hundred."

"How did you come up with that number?"

All four of my companions eagerly await my answer. This was a question that I myself had deliberated over during the past few months. I first figured that I'd lose a golf ball every ten shots. But when it turned out that I'd need more than a thousand golf balls, I revised my estimate to one lost ball every twenty shots. This produced a more reasonable number: five hundred. There's a technical term for this estimating methodology that I used to use when I worked on construction projects: it's called "pulling it out of your ass."

I shift my seat position slightly and pronounce that "it was based on the average distance of a three-iron and the probability of losing a ball measured over the entire distance of the country." I may have convinced them that I knew what I was doing, but it was clear in my own mind that this crucial calculation would only be seriously tested once I actually got out there and started golfing. And that I was putting a lot of faith into this derriere-extracted number.

Lena asks if I've ever done anything like this before. "I've been traveling for most of the past two years and I've done a lot of camping and hiking before, but never anything this big." It's a political answer that just covers my own worries about this adventure. The truth is that I'm not a veteran expeditioner. I know a little about hiking and camping from my weekend trips into the White Mountains of New Hampshire when I was young, but I'd never hiked for more than a few days. I'd certainly never attempted anything that required this much planning or effort. I wasn't even a Boy Scout, for God's sake. The questioning begins to make me uneasy. I'm getting closer to the front of the line for that imaginary roller coaster, and I think my heartbeat just increased.

I'm grateful when Alain changes the subject and points out that we're passing by the Great Wall. The five of us peer out through the dirty windows and squint into the sunlight to catch a glimpse of the historic rock pile. It's been claimed that the Great Wall of China is the only man-made object visible from space. It certainly is an impressive work of construction, even if the space visibility claim is a bit exaggerated. It snakes over every mountain and across every valley for nearly three thousand miles. It was the Strategic Defense Initiative of its day and probably cost as much in ancient dollars as modern "Star Wars" plans. The Wall was built for one reason—to keep out the violent, pillaging, looting tribes from the north, including the Mongolians. It's hard to believe that the people from this small geopolitically irrelevant nation were once so feared. But upon examining them face to face, it's not hard to believe that they would have been fierce warriors in their time.

The Mongolians are taller and broader than any other people in Asia. They look Asian with straight black hair, pale brown skin, and narrowed eyes, but their stature is more imposing. It's not unusual to see a six-foot-tall Mongolian man. Their national sports are not ping-pong and badminton, they're wrestling and horse-racing. Mongolians don't eat vegetables and rice, they eat meat. Mongolians don't ride motor scooters, they ride horses. If I were the Chinese, I probably would've built a wall, too.

On the top bunk of our tiny compartment, I sleep restlessly through the night as Chinese and Mongolian border officials inspect our passports and make us fill out the SARS questionnaire again. In the morning, it's hard to tell what was real and what was a dream, as I recollect Chinese doctors dressed in Level Three haz-ardous waste gear shuffling in and out of our compartment taking our temperatures by shoving thermometers under our armpits. I do remember waiting for what seemed like hours for the cabin attendants to unlock the door to the toilet while we were stopped at the border. On the door of the toilet, an explanation was written— "No Occupying While Stabling."

Full dissertations could be written on "Chinglish," the official translations from Chinese into English that are found throughout the country, especially near tourist attractions. I won't go into any more detail except to tell you my favorite example. A sign posted in front of a freshly seeded lawn in a city park was probably meant to say "keep off the grass." Instead, it conjured up images of a possible new border crossing. It read "No Entrance to Greenland."

Officially, I've now made it across one of China's existing borders into Mongolia and, as the sun rises, Sam and I decide to head to the restaurant car for a look at the menu. I'm surprised to see the car full so early in the morning; as I look around, I see that the women are drinking beer for breakfast and the men are drinking vodka. Everyone is putting away piles of mutton, noodles, and potatoes. I like these people.

We decide to join them in a breakfast beer and order two tall cans of Hite, a watery Korean lager which I've taken to calling "Shite." We're both confident enough in our manhood to pass on the vodka. As Sam trounces me in several games of backgammon, we stare out the window at the vast rolling grasslands of the Mongolian steppe. I feel encouraged at the sight of the short grass stretching as far as I can see. Maybe I actually *can* golf across this country.

"That's what I'm talking about!" I say excitedly, pointing to the giant natural golf course out the window. I'm trying to convince myself as much as my new acquaintance.

"Yer frickin' nuts, mate. How about another lager?"

A young Mongolian man leans over to our table and introduces himself. I thought he said his name was Bogey, which the golfer in me took as a very inauspicious sign. It turns out his name is Mogie, and he's returning home after studying in Denver, Colorado, for the past year. I tell him of my plan.

"If you need anything while in Ulaan Baatar, you can call me," he says as he hands me his home and cell phone numbers. It was exactly this kind of hospitality that made me fall in love with Mongolia on my first visit here in 2001 and what has now drawn me back for this quest to see the land in its entirety.

I know that over the next four months I'll rely heavily on the generosity of the Mongolian people. I'll be alone walking across the countryside and if the weather, illness, or any other misfortune happens to strike me, I'll need their help.

"It's all about pars, not SARS," I joke with Mogie and give him a solid handshake. His friendliness has helped lift some of my worries; it has made me feel confident that I can make it across the country. He has made me feel welcome. It's good to be in Mongolia.

Swack. I look up in search of the ball as my three-iron swings in an arc over my left shoulder and my hands vibrate uncomfortably, shocked by the sting of a leaden shot. The cold air and frigid wind compound the pain, which reverberates from the palms of my hands, gripped tightly around the club, up into my forearms. It's a deep, arthritic pain that all weekend duffers are familiar with: the feeling of a bad stroke. Imagine whacking an aluminum baseball bat against a tree, and you get the idea. The shot was a shank, a slice, a dying quail, a foul ball off the fists down the first-base line when the crowd was poised for a home run. The pain hurts, but the emotional disappointment stings even more. This, of all the golf shots in my life, was supposed to be special. This was the first stroke on the first hole of Golf Mongolia. And it was a dud.

So I'm hardly surprised when I catch sight of the white dot slicing low above the ground far right of where I aimed. "Where did it go?" asks Alain. Thankfully, he had missed the unimpressive trajectory of the ball while peering through the lens of a small Kodak point-and-shoot camera, capturing my historic swing on film. I point my club toward a patch of dirt near a telephone pole. "Over there," I reply. "I shanked it." Alain may or may not know the meaning of the word "shank." He's from Belgium and has never played golf. Not that there's anything wrong with that, but his command of English golf terminology is not proficient enough to converse about shanks, slices, pooches, and worm-burners. I'm just hoping he didn't shank the momentous photograph. "Did you get a good picture?" I'm disappointed with my poor performance, but I cheer up when I realize that the photo will only show my swing, not the unimpressive result. It may even turn out to be a photographic work of beauty, the club bending with the force of my swing just as it makes contact with the ball on the tee.

Alain is fiddling with his camera, and from the look on his face it seems possible that he may have missed the swing entirely. "I don't know! This camera sucks," he replies. "I better take a few more of your next couple shots."

"You weren't thinking about that waitress, were you?" I tease.

Alain had spent most of last night drooling over a stunningly attractive Mongolian lass who served us dinner in the restaurant of the Kherlen Hotel. "You should go see her again tonight," I suggest. "I think she liked you. She did pick all that meat out of your soup for you." Alain's a vegetarian and made the mistake of thinking that the vegetable soup he ordered would be meatless. What he failed to realize was that every Mongolian meal must include meat, and that the term "vegetable soup" means only that a few token vegetables accompany the chunks of fatty mutton swimming in the broth. The waitress appeared confused when Alain complained about the meat, but she saved the situation by taking the soup back to the kitchen and, like a true heroine, plucking every glob and morsel of animal product from the steaming bowl. Alain was either too shy to complain again or completely smitten by love, for he quickly abandoned his vegetarian principles and slurped up a spoonful of the grease-laden broth. If I hadn't almost wet myself laughing, I might have even thought it was romantic.

"Oh, piss off!" he shoots back as I bend down, swing my backpack up onto my shoulders, and begin walking. "You're just jealous."

My long journey has begun. My backpack is filled with fifty-five pounds of gear, food, and balls, and I take short, steady steps over the green and brown grass clumps that struggle to cover the barren earth, like patches of fur on a mangy dog. It feels good to be walking and on my way after months of planning, shank be damned.

The three-iron, which for the next several months will double as my walking stick (maybe even as a weapon, should trouble arise), swings in my right hand as we depart the first tee and head onto the fairway of my two-million-yard golf course. Just behind us looms the Mongolian Heroes' Memorial, which features a bronze statue of a man on horseback, his outstretched arm stabbing the air with a sword. An aging Soviet tank sits beside the statue, and surrounding these two icons is a twelve-foot-high semicircular wall covered with murals of soldiers in battle, farmers working the land, and factory workers laboring. These are the heroes the Memorial celebrates, and the images of idealism under Mongolia's Communist Party. Much has changed since 1990, when the Soviet Union began to collapse and Mongolia broke its ties with its iron-fisted Big Brother to the north. Like me, Mongolia has embarked on a great journey. With communism as its caddy, Mongolia shot bogey golf in the twentieth century, missing many targets of prosperity for its citizens. Now, with capitalism guiding its shots, Mongolia has completely changed its swing, and is struggling for a way to save par. Strolling down the fairway on the outskirts of Choibalsan, a decrepit city struggling to maintain its vitality in the post-Soviet age, evidence of change is everywhere.

The memorial is located near Choibalsan's drama theater and two museums. The area once bustled with activity but has now gone to seed. The abandoned buildings that ring the neighborhood are being slowly torn apart for construction materials. Few people live here in this forgotten corner of the city, and the only visitors appear to be locals scavenging for materials—or wayward travelers in search of golf balls. The area was meant to be an epicenter of the city's culture, modeled in the European fashion. But today, Choibalsan's residents have no time for heroic memorials left over from the Soviet propaganda machine. Instead, they struggle to survive the new Big Brother, capitalism, as Mongolia, like so many developing nations, searches for prosperity and identity in a world dominated by Western culture. Trade with China, Korea, and Japan slowly replaces the vacuum left by the departure of Soviet commercial activity in this eastern Mongolian trade hub. This part of the city gives me the creeps, and it reminds me of a burned-out urban nightmare from a postapocalyptic movie. Located near Mongolia's eastern border, Choibalsan seemed the logical starting point for my journey when I espied the city on maps. As Alain and I walk away from the memorial, however, I almost wish I had chosen a more uplifting location to tee off. I can't wait to get the hell out of this place.

Then I spot my ball, a paltry 120 yards from where I hit it. It's a relief to find the ball so easily. I drop my backpack to the ground with a thud and glance over at Alain, who stands a few meters away. "Are you ready?" I shout. I'd like him to get a few more good photos, just in case *National Geographic* comes calling. After dinking my last shot, a solid hit would be nice, and I concentrate on the fundamentals of a good golf swing. At the top of my backswing

I drive my hips forward, shifting my body weight to the front leg and pulling the club through the ball. Just as I make contact, the shutter clicks. Perfect. This time, the center of my club head, the "sweet spot," smacks the ball dead on, and it rockets off toward the concrete foundation of a crumbling building. There's nothing like the feeling of a solid hit, which, unlike the previous shank, sends a shiver of excitement through my body. "That's more like it!" I yell. It's the best that I could hope for from my three-iron, more than two hundred yards and perfectly straight. I'll be in good shape if I can continue with shots like that one. Alain and I march again across the grass, heading due west toward my ball.

This one is harder to find. Unlike a freshly mowed and mani-cured golf course with lush, inch-high Kentucky bluegrass, my "fairway" consists of gravelly sand covered with a patchwork of dry or dead prairie grass, unruly weeds, and spidery ground cover. I drop my pack and walk in slow concentric circles around it, scan-ning the surface for a trace of a little white ball. "Find it yet?" I shout to Alain, hoping he will help me locate the ball. He's not only the team cameraman for the day; he's also my ball spotter. Although at the moment he's doing a piss-poor job of it. Finally, he shouts, "Here it is!" He's standing about fifty yards in front of me. I had grossly underestimated the length of my shot. This concerns me, but I'm happy that I didn't lose my first ball after only two shots, so I lift my backpack up onto my right hip as I step another fifty yards toward Alain, who is smiling. His look of amusement concerns me, for it resembles the way pals will laugh at one another's misfortune in a gleeful "you're soooo screwed!" sort of way.

The ball is buried under a patch of creeping thick-stemmed weeds. I use my three-iron to drag the ball a couple feet to the left. "Are you allowed to do that?" Alain asks suspiciously, disappointed that he won't be able to see me flail into the weeds. "Of course I am," I respond. I'm playing by what golfers call "winter rules," which means I can take a preferred lie within one club length of the spot where the ball rests. It may sound unsportsmanlike, but let's be serious for a moment. Golfing across an entire nation will be difficult enough without having to hack my way out of the depths of a weed patch or off of rocks and other hazards. Taking a preferred lie is extremely reasonable under these circumstances. Besides, it's June and I'm freezing my ass off, so "winter rules" seem even more appropriate. And there's another practical reason: My three-iron is a sturdy tool, with a steel shaft and forged iron head, but golf clubs do break if misused, and this is the only one I've got. This club must survive the longest and perhaps the most arduous round of golf ever conceived. I explain these rules to Alain and go even further by stating that "this is my expedition and I can make whatever damn rules I want." A hint of indignation tinges my voice, unsettled that my only companion would question my integrity. Alain settles for the explanation, then readies the camera.

Again, it is another solid hit. "Nice one, André!" shouts Alain as we watch my third shot sail toward the horizon. It's another two-hundred-yard beauty, and the ball hangs high and spins into the air until a wind gust knocks it down violently and to the left. "Thanks," I reply in the soft-spoken way that proud golfers do when their playing partners offer a compliment. I lift the back-pack to my shoulders once again, and we walk forward beneath a gray overcast sky. One or two more shots and I'll be away from the last traces of the city, the ruins of dilapidated buildings and piles of garbage that dot this eerie landscape. It's not just the unsightly nature of this neighborhood that bothers me; the golfing is more difficult here because of the unnatural features present on the land. Ruts from truck tires collect drifting dry grass, and scattered bits of white-colored trash act like golf ball decoys, leading me astray. It'll be much better once I get away from the city.

It's hard to say many nice things about Choibalsan, capital of Dornod *aimag*, Mongolia's easternmost province. There is almost no vegetation inside the city limits, and the spaces around the bland, rectangular concrete buildings are covered in bare sandy dirt. The aging four-story apartment buildings where most people live in the city were built in the Soviet style. They are simple, unadorned, util-itarian living spaces, whose concrete facades also happen to be the color of sand. In a word, it is drab. I spent only one full day in Choibalsan, and the Siberian winds that whipped dust into my eyes hardly made me feel warm and welcomed. Then again, it's hard to expect much hospitality from a city named for a mass murderer.

Pre-1990 history books likely depict Khorloogiyn Choibalsan as a hero of the nation's independence movement during the 1920s. From 1928 to 1952, he ruled the country, defending its sovereignty while maintaining a delicate balance of autonomy and allegiance with the Soviet Union. But with their newfound freedom of press and speech since 1990, many Mongolian scholars have documented Choibalsan's more disturbing legacy. As a disciple of Joseph Stalin, he followed the same ruthless tactics as his mentor and quashed all dissent or criticism of his rule. Choibalsan killed more than thirty thousand people, mostly monks and scholars, during mass purges in the 1930s. In short, he's not the kind of guy you'd want to criticize if he hit a bad drive off the first tee. But Choibalsan is long gone, and, as his statue fades away from my view, I gladly march away from the ruins of his city and toward the open skies of the countryside.

I spot my ball after a few minutes of searching. It rests behind a volleyball-size tumbleweed that I sweep away with my golf club. I bend down and prop the ball up on a tuft of dry grass that should allow me to get my club under the ball enough to get it airborne. Whoosh. The wispy grass flies as I swing, and stroke number four is another good shot of about two hundred yards, the average distance I must maintain if I'm to achieve this course's par of 11,880. Again, I hoist my heavy pack to my shoulders and trek toward the ball. The weight of the pack is burdensome, but it also brings some comfort. My challenges in the preparation of this expedition have mostly been mental. I've debated, discussed, and deliberated over all the details: the course, the gear, which club to use. I've talked up a good game to everyone I've met. But now it's time for action, and it feels good to have the burden shift from my mind to my legs. After all the headaches associated with preparing for the trip, I look forward to some old-fashioned physical exertion.

My fourth shot flew toward a distant bend in the river and I pace in that direction. But as I draw nearer, I notice a steep embankment that had been impossible to see from a distance. Without yardage markers or flagsticks to guide me, judging the landing area of my shots is difficult in this flat, featureless landscape. I hesitate, debating whether I should look for my ball on the top or bottom of the hill. Alain's unlikely to offer me any worthwhile advice in this search, so I hedge my bets and leave my bag at the top of the hill and descend into a quagmire of knee-high spiny weeds. After five minutes of trouncing through the knee-high growth, I throw in the towel. "It's lost," I confess to Alain.

"So, what do you do now?" he asks.

"I'll drop another one," I reply, unzipping the top pocket of my backpack. Alain's silence is respectful, as if he had just seen my pet dog get run over by a car.

This is a milestone—my first lost ball. Although a lost ball can be a tragic event for most golfers, I'm secretly a little bit happy to be lightening the load in my backpack by 1.6 ounces. Of the 500 golf balls I brought to Mongolia, 150 of them, weighing fifteen pounds, are in my pack. I stashed the rest, along with my four-iron, at

Nassan's guest house in Ulaan Baatar, where the staff promised to look after them for me. I'll pass through there one-third of the way through my journey to collect the remaining balls before heading west to play the final twelve holes. I reach into the top pocket of my backpack and pull out a new "distance" golf ball. I have an assortment of brands represented in my bag that together make up the pantheon of the cheap golf ball world. All the biggest golf ball companies refused me when I asked for a courtesy supply of their finest balls in the form of a sponsorship. So instead, I walked out of Discount Sport Mart with a shopping cart full of the cheapest balls money could buy. To hell with 'em. I don't need their super-spinning, balata-covered, new-and-improved technology golf balls, anyway. I just need distance, and my swing will provide what's needed for that.

My fifth shot grabs 220 yards of this distance. After twenty minutes of walking and several swings, my body temperature is rising and my golf game is getting into a good groove. "How much longer are you going to walk with me?" I ask Alain. "I'll go up to that ridge with you near those cows, and then I'll follow the river back to town," he replies. I'm unsettled by the thought of his departure. As well as being a volunteer photographer and the only witness to the beginning of my adventure, he's become a good friend.

Like I said, we met each other on the train from Beijing to Ulaan Baatar and, for the past several days, he's been my sounding board as I've made all the last-minute decisions before beginning my solo

journey. When he mentioned that he was interested in accompanying me to this remote eastern city, I suggested that he surely must
have something better to do. But I wanted the company, so I didn't
discourage him further, although I'm not sure if he was genuinely
swept up by the excitement of the world's first cross-country golf
expedition, or if he wanted to witness the beginning of a tragic tale
of failure. Or maybe he really did have nothing better to do.

He's been traveling for three months from Belgium to Pakistan
by bus and train, and now he's returning to Europe via China,
Mongolia, and Russia. In the thousands of miles he's traveled,
though, no single journey has been as painful or miserable as the
twenty-hour ride we shared in a Russian minivan from Ulaan
Baatar to Choibalsan.

That voyage began two days ago, when Alain and I arrived at
the Ulaan Baatar eastern bus depot at 6:00 A.M. and found our way
onto a Choibalsan-bound van filling with passengers and cargo. I
counted twelve seats, but eighteen other passengers with their luggage had already laid claim to a tiny piece of real estate inside the
van, and they encouraged Alain and me to do the same. The driver
hovered around the van, chatting with other drivers before disappearing for over an hour while we waited inside the sardine tin. He
returned to collect the fare of 10,000 tögrögs (1100 tögrögs equals
$1) from each passenger. He asked Alain and me for 15,000,
explaining that we had backpacks with us so we should pay more.
It was a brazen attempt to extort additional money from stupid

foreigners, plain and simple, and we objected. I pointed out that we each had one backpack while most of the other passengers had dozens of boxes and suitcases, many of which occupied the space where my legs should go. If anything, we should pay less! The driver protested meekly, but took our money and shut up— although he got the last laugh, disappearing for another hour before returning to start the engine.

After a ten-minute ride through the dusty slums of Ulaan Baatar's ger suburbs, shantytowns of canvas and felt, we pulled up to a shack surrounded by oil drums and skeletons of Russian-made jeeps and vans. The driver got out and began talking to a grease-covered teenaged boy. The two of them walked around the building and out of sight from our humanity-filled, cargo-stuffed van where the temperature had risen significantly. Where was he going now?

Forty-five minutes later he returned, holding an oily black engine part, and it became clear: the van needed some last-minute repairs. It was already 11:00 A.M., and the morning sun baked the van. I panted and tried to remain calm. Why hadn't he taken care of these errands before?

By noon, he had finished the mechanical work and filled the tank with gas in another remote corner of the city, and then we were finally on our way.

As if the body heat from the twenty passengers inside the van wasn't bad enough, I had the seat directly over the engine compartment. This not only meant that I had no legroom, but also that there was a near-scalding hot metal extrusion that I had to straddle or risk melting the soles off my boots. I tried to lift my feet up onto the back of the front seat during the beginning of the journey but this infuriated the driver, so I placed them intermittently on the engine cover or on top of the feet of Alain or the woman squeezed in next to me. My knees begged to be stretched, and I grew more and more anxious as we crawled along at twenty miles per hour on the bumpy, potholed dirt-track excuse for a road. I grew desperate with discomfort. I just had to stretch my legs. I tried one more time to place my feet up but the driver yelled at me again. How much longer would I be able to take this? Alain's face was pale and unexpressive. He looked like a tortured prisoner who had given up all hope. Then I felt a tap on my shoulder.

Three young men sitting behind us had broken out a bottle of Arkhi vodka. *Arkhi* means "liquor," or "spirits," in Mongolian, and it would be impossible to find a more generic brand name for a Mongolian vodka than Arkhi. At less than two dollars per bottle, it might also be impossible to find a cheaper brand. The young men lacked a cup to drink it from, so they removed a plastic ashtray from one of the van's armrests and filled it with the rotgut liquid and leaned forward, dangling the noxious liquid in front of my face. Under any other circumstance, I would have refused the proffered potable; but with an enormous distance yet to travel, I grabbed the little tray and downed the vodka, grimacing. I dug through my belongings and found a few Valium pills that I had bought in Myanmar a year earlier. I had no chance to escape the van, so I popped a pill and offered one to Alain, hoping for a chemical-induced serenity.

Four hours later, we stopped alongside the road on the open steppe for a bathroom break, and I approached one of the vodka-drinking boys who spoke some broken English. I asked him to translate to the driver that I didn't mean to be disrespectful, but that the metal plate over the engine was burning my feet and it was so crowded that I had nowhere else to put them. The translated reply came back as follows: "He said you can sit in the back with the luggage if you want." The boy motioned with a sideways lean of his head to the tiny space behind the last seat where bags and boxes were jammed from floor to ceiling.

"Tell him he can go fuck himself," I replied, "if he wants." The boy didn't need to translate: my tone was clear. Needless to say, my relationship with the driver soured into one of mutual antagonism after that. I was tired and miserable, and this guy had really pissed me off.

As evening approached, a city appeared on the horizon. "We've been driving at least ten hours," I told Alain. "This must be Choibalsan." As he dug through his backpack for a map, we passed an enormous sign that spelled out the name of the city in Cyrillic: Öndörkhaan. "No, this *can't* be Öndörkhaan," Alain said in disbelief. "That would mean we're only halfway there." The Arkhi was long gone, so I dug out another Valium and swallowed it dry.

As night fell, the nightmare continued. The driver got lost and had to backtrack across the steppe to find the road again. I silently gloated and called him an idiot under my breath. He shifted his gaze from the road to my reflection in the rear-view mirror occasionally, staring disdainfully. This trip was bringing out the worst in me. My feet burned, my knees hurt, the Valium and vodka bleared my thoughts but failed to knock me out, and my patience was about to snap. Unable to sleep, I bobbed along in a semiconscious state throughout the night until, finally, the van stopped. We had run out of gas.

The first light of dawn had begun to paint the morning sky as I stumbled out of the van, stretched my legs and tried to regain my sanity. I unpacked my three-iron and took a few practice swings on some dried horse dung. The morning was completely silent except for the wind riffling through the grass. I looked to the horizon in all directions but could see no evidence of human habitation. Mongolia is a vast land of big skies and empty spaces. Alone, a man could wander for weeks without meeting another soul. Can I really golf across this country? I wondered. Swinging my three-iron relaxed me, even if the horse turds exploded on contact. This van ride will be over soon, I told myself. Then the real trip will begin.

An hour later, a rescue party arrived in the form of another passenger van. The drivers laughed while siphoning gas between the two vehicles, giving the impression that this kind of thing happens all the time. I squeezed back into my seat, still clutching my golf club, and we crawled off once again toward the distant city of Choibalsan.

I could see the outskirts of the city in the early morning sunlight when the van suddenly stopped again. I thought it was an unusual time for a toilet break, but I climbed out over the boxes that were piled in front of the door and stepped outside for a whiz. One of the young men had woken from his vodka-induced stupor and stood next to me, also relieving himself. There was some discussion in the van and the boy turned to me and laughed, "We ran out of gas again." I almost stopped in midstream.

Thirty minutes later, another van rescued us with a few liters of gas and we finally covered the last five miles into the center of the city. As we passed by the Kherlen Hotel, a gray rectangle of concrete, I leaned into the front seat and asked the driver to let us out. We pulled our backpacks out from the back of the van, and as we said good-bye to everyone, I found myself eye to eye with the driver. It was a frustrating and shitty ride for him, too, and neither of us had any energy left for contempt. I said good-bye cheerfully, and he stuck out his arm. We shook hands.

A day later, the trip is still fresh in my memory as Alain and I search for my ball. "Hey, maybe you'll get the same asshole van driver on the way back," I mention to Alain. He looks down and shakes his head. "Yeah, but maybe the girl from the restaurant will be sitting next to me this time, instead of your fat ass."

I spot a flash of white among some dead foliage and rush over to investigate. It's my ball, though I seem to have misjudged the distance on this one by a good twenty yards. Searching for the ball has been the worst part of the day. Though I've spotted some right away, others have taken up to five minutes to find. My swing feels good and I yearn to hit the ball repeatedly, without the annoying search missions. I stare ahead in the distance to get a feeling about whether the upcoming terrain will be any more golf-friendly. Cows graze to the left of me in the tall grass near the river, so I avoid them and the higher grass by altering my course to follow a barren ridge to the right. It looks more golfable. As luck would have it, this turns out to be a wise decision and I lose no balls for the next ten shots.

"Well, good luck." Alain reaches out his arms and embraces me. He had walked with me for over an hour and witnessed the first thirteen shots of the expedition, and even documented it with photographs. But it's time to part. This is my journey, and I must be prepared to complete it on my own, despite how much I'd love to have someone with me. "Don't worry, you'll be fine on your own," he says. "The Mongolians will take good care of you."

It's reassuring, but I can't help being a tad jealous of him. He's going to spend the night in the comfort and safety of the Kherlen Hotel in downtown Choibalsan, and tomorrow he'll be on a van headed back toward Ulaan Baatar. The van ride is nothing to look forward to, but at least his immediate future is certain, while mine is filled with the unknown. There are so many things that I haven't thought out completely. What if I run out of golf balls? What if my tent and sleeping bag aren't warm enough? What if I get harassed or robbed by strangers? What if I get seriously ill or hurt myself? How will I get help?

"Stay in touch," I say, and he lifts his hand in one final wave before marching off in the opposite direction. The real moment of truth has arrived. Fighting off loneliness will be one of the greatest challenges of the coming weeks and months, and the fight has just begun. I turn around and focus on the little white ball in front of me.

After seventy-two respectable golf shots, I'm unable to lift my backpack on and off my shoulders one more time. I drop the pack to the ground and sit beside it. The wind has blown steadily, and I fear that I haven't reached my goal of fifteen kilometers today. But there's no way I can continue. I'm exhausted. I dig into the top pocket of my bag and remove my GPS receiver. In the few seconds it takes for the device to get a clear signal from the satellites, I try to guess how far I've golfed—twelve, maybe fourteen kilometers. A misguided optimism leads me to believe it'll be fourteen, while my better judgment says, "No, be real, it can't be more than twelve." I stare intently at the handheld device, like an addicted gambler watching the wheels spin on a slot machine. When it shows a "ready to navigate" message, I push a sequence of buttons to display the distance I've traveled. Ten point three. This is bad news.

I'm hoping to average fifteen to twenty kilometers per day (nine to thirteen miles). At that pace, I'll reach the finish line in the city of Khovd in about four months. Any slower and I'll be caught in the freezing temperatures of the harsh Mongolian winter, which descends upon the land in early October. My first day is a bit of a disappointment in this regard, but I set up my tent and crawl inside, happy to have finished the day with only five lost balls. Tomorrow I'll be refreshed and get a full day of golfing in. Maybe I'll even do twenty kilometers. I can hear the rushing waters of the Kherlen River nearby, and, as my tent shakes in the gusting wind, I fall asleep.

When I wake, night has not yet fallen. In the summer, sunset comes between nine and ten o'clock in Mongolia, and I take advantage of this comforting twilight to walk down to the riverbank to replenish my water supply. This is the first time I've used my water filter, and I dunk the end of the plastic inlet tube into the rushing brown water. With downward pressure I pump the handle of the filter and watch as a steady trickle of clear water drops down into my Chinese water bottle. It's a little trickle of magic: silty, cow piss–contaminated liquid turning into potable, life-sustaining water, and I stop halfway through for a few swallows of the cold fluid.

I opt for a pasta-and-bouillon-cube dinner and fire up my lightweight, multi-fuel cookstove on a patch of bare dirt near my tent, kicking away a few cow patties. The flame roars like a tiny jet engine in the wind. My gear is all working properly, despite my failure to test any of it before the trip began. So far, luck has been on my side. Perhaps I can pull this off.

In my deep exhaustion-induced sleep this night, I dream of reaching the eigteenth hole and reveling in the success of my expedition. How could I have known that while I slept, the ferocious northerly winds and eastward-flowing Kherlen River were conspiring against me to give the expedition its first serious test?

It's day six of the expedition and my body is rebelling. Since my rolling-tent escapade and subsequent river adventure on day two, I've hit over a hundred shots a day, averaged nearly a 190 yards per swing, and walked nearly twenty kilometers each day. My progress is good, exactly what I need to finish the expedition before winter. But there is no joy in my tent tonight. No celebrations, no dancing—and, most important, not a trace of optimism. Instead, I sit alone and emotionless. My back aches, my hands hurt, and my feet throb from the acres of blisters covering their soles.

My thumb flicks the tiny metal wheel of a pink cigarette lighter that I bought in an Ulaan Baatar kiosk, and, with a satisfying click, a small orange flame pokes up like a jack-in-the-box. The flame illuminates my tent in the dwindling twilight. With my right hand, I hold my Swiss Army knife over the flame and scald the blade to sterilize it. Then, I move the blade toward my bare feet, take a deep breath, and slice into my skin. I'm not sure if this is wise or not, but I feel like I must do something; the blisters are becoming unbearable. They've grown for the past five days like unwanted mushrooms in the Royal Gardens. Blobby, white masses that have doubled in size nearly every day until now, they almost cover the soles of my feet. The time has come for action, and without medical consultation available, I do what I think is best. Methodically, I draw the hot knife blade across each baggy node of skin and dab the open incisions with a small wad of toilet paper to soak up the oozing yellow fluid.

It feels good. My troubles seem to be flowing away in that tiny river of pus, soon to be thrown away with the white tissue paper. Tomorrow, I hope, I'll be able to walk without pain again. But now, I'm hit with a faint memory like a pebble tossed at my skull. And the memory says, "Salt." "Put salt on blisters," the tiny voice says, "it dries them up." It's an experienced hiker who I've met somewhere in my past who is speaking. "Salt," he says again. Damn, who is that? The ding on my head from the little pebble has faded away, and now I'm left wondering if I really met someone who told me about salt or if I'm just imagining the whole thing. I sit for a moment with the ball of toilet paper in my hand, staring at the zip-top bag that contains my Band-Aids and antibiotic ointment. I had planned to apply the ointment and bandages and let the healing begin, but now I'm wondering about salt. I push aside my bag of medical supplies and from my backpack, I withdraw a plastic bag containing, among other spices and condiments, a large bag of salt.

"Owwww! Shit! Crap!" That was stupid. What the hell was I thinking? Salt in an open wound? Of course it stings! I may as well have stuck my tongue on a frozen lamp post. "God, that was dumb!" Clenching my teeth, I quickly spread some triple antibiotic ointment over the lightly salted meat and then cover the wounds with a layer of gauze and several pieces of white adhesive tape. I pull my crunchy, dried sweat–laden socks back onto my feet and lie down on top of my sleeping bag.

Stretched out flat on my back, with the effects of the minor surgery and salt torture on my feet dissipating, I organize the various maladies my body possesses into a hierarchy of pain. The feet are definitely the worst. Not only do the blisters burn my soles with every step, but a more generalized soreness has permeated them. This, I'm guessing, comes from the altered walking stance I've adopted. I've compensated for the blisters on my insteps by gingerly limping along on the outsides of my feet, and now each entire foot hurts equally.

Second on the pain list is my back. Six days ago in Choibalsan, Alain lifted my backpack. "Wow, that's heavy! Are you sure you can manage?"

"No, I'm not sure. In fact, that damn backpack is so heavy that I can't possibly think I'll be able to lift it on and off my shoulders a hundred times a day. I'm an idiot for even beginning the expedition like this, but you see I've come this far and I'm not turning back now. So don't ask any more stupidly obvious questions, you dipshit!"

That's what I should have said. Instead, I offered up a lame reply, hiding the truth and my worst fears like an ostrich burying his head in the sand. An ostrich with a fifty-five-pound backpack on his shoulders. "No problem," I said. "I'm tough; I can handle it."

Six days later, I'm not so sure that I can handle it. That godforsaken backpack is heavy. It's not only full of all my survival gear (tent, sleeping bag, stove, water filter, etc.), but there's food inside, plus two and a half liters (read five and a half pounds) of water, and most ridiculously of all—more than ten pounds of golf balls. Pain radiates from my neck all the way down my back every time I lift the burden up onto my shoulders. Every step across the grass is an excruciating effort, and with every step I'm thinking about how much it hurts; it's getting harder and harder to concentrate on the golf. As I get progressively more tired throughout the day, I hit poorer golf shots. And every bad shot means a shorter distance until I have to heave the backpack on and off again. Which means more heaving, which, in turn, tires me out more, causing me to hit more bad shots. It's a downward spiraling abyss of self-destruction into which I'm headed, and it's hard to see a way out.

Third on the pain list are the blisters on my hands from

swinging the golf club. What can I say? Am I really going to bitch about how much my hands hurt from playing too much golf? No.

Well, yes. I've got Band-Aids on four of my eight fingers and on one thumb. Beneath the little pink strips of fabric lie open patches of torn pink flesh. I don't expect any sympathy. It's a golf expedition, after all. But an ounce of understanding wouldn't hurt, even if it is my own fault.

I don't wear a golf glove. Many golfers do, including most of the professionals. But I'm part of a minority, like people who take the bus to work instead of driving, who still prefer the natural feel of the club in our hands when we play. It's the simple low-tech approach to the game. But playing without a glove has its disadvantages: the club can slip if it's just a little wet, in cold weather there's no insulation to dampen bad vibrations from the club, and, most important, blisters tend to form more easily. Normally I play often enough that calluses form on my hands. But I've only played golf twice in the past three years.

I know what you're thinking. He's only played *twice* in the past *three years?* The guy golfing across Mongolia is not a maniacally obsessed golfer? He's not a professional who makes his living from the game? Actually, in my world-backpacking sojourn, which has taken up two and a half years, I've put golf aside in favor of exploring remote corners of the globe. Even so, one of those two rounds of golf was at the La Paz Country Club in Bolivia. Not only is that course situated among the beautiful karst scenery of the

Valley of the Moon, but it is also allegedly the highest golf course in the world. The ball flies easily through the thin atmosphere when you're playing at more than two miles above sea level, and I'll always remember that round of golf for the three-hundred-yard drives that I nonchalantly boomed of the tees. My other round was at a charity tournament in Los Angeles a month ago. That was the extent of my preparation for a two-million-yard golf expedition that stretches from one end of a nation to the other. Now that I think of it, a few more practice rounds might have been in order.

But the quality of my swing is much less of a concern than the quantity of blisters on my hands, and tonight, for the first time since I started walking six days ago, I'm thinking about quitting. I struggle with this thought and its full ramifications. Am I going to go down in history as a quitter? Will I be known as the man who *couldn't* golf across Mongolia? It's a depressing thought, and I wish I had someone to talk things over with, someone to help guide me in this decision. But I'm alone. As I've been for most of the past six days. The only human contact I had today was when three men yelled to me while I was searching for my thirty-fifth shot of the day at around 11:00 A.M.

The men waved their arms in the air and motioned for me to come toward them. I abandoned the search for my ball and slowly marched in their direction. Two of the men were wearing button-down dress shirts and jeans with black rubber boots pulled up high, and one was wearing a *deel,* the traditional wool overcoat worn by most Mongolians. Their lean faces were dark from exposure to the sun, and all had the tousled look of men who work hard as a daily routine. My Mongolian language skills were good enough to perceive that they said *"sain bainuu"* (hello), but that's all I could decipher. I replied with a "sain bainuu" of my own before noticing the object of their attention. A cow.

The cow must have been either sick or injured and was half-submerged in the water at the bottom of a steep riverbank. The men had managed to get a few ropes around the beast, but the three of them couldn't quite drag it up the slope, and this was where I was needed. A few minutes earlier, I had been limping around on my blistered feet looking for a golf ball, complaining to myself about how much my backpack weighed, and now I was being asked, by three strangers who didn't speak my language, to drag a cow up a riverbank. What could I say? I grabbed an end of the rope.

Two of us heaved and struggled with the ropes while the other two pushed on the bovine flesh. The animal was clearly unhappy, and a load of fresh manure sprayed out of its tail end. The thin rope dug into the blisters on my hands as I pulled, but I wasn't about to let go. Mongolians have always been generous and helpful to me wherever I have traveled in their country, and here was an opportunity for me to give something back. Besides, these guys were tough, and I didn't want to act like a wimp and run away crying about my hands. I had my manly pride and the reputation of all Western men to consider. I dug my boots into the soft mud of the steep riverbank and leaned back, heaving with all my strength on the ropes.

After five minutes of pulling, shoving, and coaxing, we managed to haul the cow to the top of the bank. The men all smiled, satisfied. One of them had gotten sprayed by the cow's bowel movement, and he looked at me and laughed as if saying, "What are you gonna do?" I laughed out loud, just as much at him as with him. Thank God it wasn't me who had gotten sprayed by the fecal blast. I only have one pair of pants with me, and it's a long way to the next Laundromat.

There wasn't much left to talk about (or mime about) after we completed the emergency cowlift, so I raised one hand and said good-bye. The men all thanked me and watched as I returned to my backpack and golf club, which I had left fifty meters away. That was the highlight of my day: helping some Mongolian dudes pull a sick cow out of a river.

Now, in the solitude of my tent, I'm evaluating my options. I could dump some golf balls to lighten the load. But this is risky: I've barely got enough to make it back to UB where my supply is stashed. On the other hand, I could dump them all and walk. It's the golf that's making my life miserable—the extra weight of the golf balls, and blisters on my hands. And without the repetitive removal and reshouldering of my backpack every two hundred yards, I'd be much better off. Especially if I dumped the extra ten pounds of balls. I'll be able to walk twenty-five kilometers per day, no problem. This is the best idea I've had yet!

Wait a minute. Whoa, hold on. It's *Golf* Mongolia, not *Walk* Mongolia. I can't *not* golf. It shouldn't even be an option. No, my fate has two possibilities, and the bleak choices are much like those of a prisoner in a forced-labor camp: I can either toil in the miserable conditions all day, or commit expedition suicide and call the whole thing off right now. If I do kill it, I'll be in a restaurant with pizza and beer in less than twenty-four hours. Now, there's a thought I can dwell on for a while. Should it be the *Pizza Funghi* or the *Quattro Staggione?* Thinking about my limited options and the immediate lack of pizza and beer in my tent is so depressing that I decide not to cook dinner tonight. Instead, I lie on top of my sleeping bag until it gets dark, and then I crawl inside until morning.

When I wake in the morning, I find that I've slept twelve hours. Sleep is the one positive thing that I have to report thus far. I've never slept so well in all my life as I have these past few days. To call it sleeping like a baby wouldn't do it justice. Babies don't walk fifteen miles a day carrying fifty-five pounds on their backs. No, this is an adult sleep. A sleep that comes from years of experience knowing what hard work is, not the naive slumber of an infant who knows little about life's difficulties. It's Man-Sleep.

Despite the faraway places I visited during the dreams of my manly slumber, I peek out through the clear plastic window in the tent's rain fly and see that I'm still in Mongolia. The sky is a solid shade of gray, as it has been for the past five days, and the wind violently rattles the loose flaps of my nylon tent. Before venturing out to the start of my journey from Ulaan Baatar, I learned from the *UB Post,* one of Mongolia's two weekly English-language newspapers, that forest fires were devouring enormous swathes of Siberian forest, just north of Mongolia. Peering at the sky now, I can see the effects. The northerly wind that has been harassing my golf game carries faint odors of burnt pine and charred fir—what I imagine to be the primary characteristics of Siberian smoke. The sky is tainted by the kind of haze that you might find hanging over an industry-filled city in a forgotten corner of Russia; but here, in the boundless nature of the Mongolian steppe, it seems out of place. It obscures the comforting warmth and light of the sun and gives the air a bitter taste. It makes me feel more and more like Frodo, in *The Lord of the Rings,* on a difficult and dangerous journey into the dark land of Mordor, with evil lurking all around. Amidst the pallid smoky atmosphere, the primary evil here is the wind, arch-enemy of every golfer.

Wind is, to a round of golf, what rain is to a day at the beach. Golfers perform hundreds of mathematical equations in their heads before every swing, finely tuning the calculations of dynamic physics and gravity. But the wind has no respect for science. It tosses out these calculations like a football player at a fraternity party throwing two nerdy mathematicians out the door. Tumbleweeds have zipped past me in the blink of an eye as I've readied myself to swing the club. I've seen my golf ball pushed around to the left and right, and back at me. Yes, this wind is evil. And the dark skies don't make me feel any more welcome.

The harsh wind is just another reason why I lie inside my sleeping bag for an extra half-hour this morning, struggling to find the motivation to endure another day of searching for golf balls in the grass while schlepping my weighty possessions around on my back all day. But then again, there's the MacCereal to look forward to.

This is my seventh breakfast alone out on the steppe, and I've had MacCereal every morning. It comes in little packets that have an American flag and a bald eagle on the front. It's all natural—just dehydrated milk, sugar, and tiny rice and corn flakes. It's meant to be eaten warm; but I can't be bothered heating up water this early in the morning, so I mix it with a swirl of cold water from my Yingxing cup. I bought a bag of twenty MacCereal packets in the State Department Store in Ulaan Baatar and I've already gone through twelve. I love the name MacCereal, and its proud representation of American consumer culture in the Mongolian marketplace. Though I have to admit it's not the best name I've seen in Mongolia: That prize belongs to a hamburger restaurant in Ulaan Baatar with golden arches in the shape of an *M*, with yellow letters on a red background spelling out the name MonRonald's.

The sugary, quick-carb breakfast gives me enough energy to pack up my tent and trudge up the hill to yesterday's finishing point, about two hundred yards away. The past few days, I've camped near the river in order to have easy access to my daily ration of water, but I've golfed along the higher ridge where the grass is shorter than in the floodplain. This strategy has worked fairly well, keeping the lost-ball count low. Today, however, it looks as though I'll have a decision to make. The river bends significantly toward the south, while my course should be heading west.

Mulling over my decision, I drop a ball and start my morning routine: a few stretches and some practice swings to loosen up the golf muscles. In the distance, a dust cloud rises from a truck barreling along the road from Choibalsan. I watch closely to gauge its direction. I know that this truck, like any truck I'm likely to see here, is headed along the main track to the next regional capital city of Öndörkhaan, and this is where I should be heading as well.

I've had no trouble figuring out where I am. I plot my GPS coordinates on my map every night, so it's unlikely that I'll ever be truly lost. But knowing exactly where to point the golf club on every shot is another story. If I follow the Kherlen River too closely, then I'll be zigzagging along with the meandering watercourse, and this will cost me time and distance. But following a road is harder than it sounds. The roads here are just dirt tracks, dozens of more or less parallel dirt tracks to be precise, and they can veer off unexpectedly toward distant towns or villages. So it's difficult to know if I'm actually crossing the main road if I hit a shot across a pair of worn tire ruts in the dry grass, or if I'm just crossing the trail to Enkhbayar and Nyamdorj's sheep farm. I've got more than a thousand miles ahead of me, and any extra deviation will cause undue psychological stress, as well as additional blisters. That's why I'm watching this truck the way Marlin

Perkins would watch a flock of migrating geese. This truck is
heading west.

Aiming toward the dissipating vehicular dust cloud, my first shot
of the day strikes the ball off-center and the club vibrates in my hand.
Underneath the Band-Aids, my blisters are already throbbing. I have
a feeling it's going to be a bad day. I lightly walk forward on my band-
aged feet. "The salt was definitely, definitely a bad idea," I think. I
can still feel a burning sensation every once in a while as I step.

Ahead of me is the Mongolian steppe. This is what I came to
conquer: thousands of miles of natural grasslands. There is not a
tree in sight. I haven't seen one, in fact, since I left Choibalsan. Just
endless rolling yellow-brown terrain, speckled with the first sprout-
ings of spring green.

With a measured application of golfer's focus, I straighten out
my second shot and it sails high through the hazy, wind-filled sky.
Then it's back to the same routine I've perfected over the past several days: lift the pack to the shoulders, snap the waist buckle, pick
up the golf club, mark my line, and begin counting my steps. One,
two, three, four, five, six, and on up to two hundred and twenty,
where I should once again find my ball.

The strategy of lining up an object on the horizon to mark the
ball's line of flight and then counting my steps has become the only
real method of giving myself a good chance at finding the ball. It's
a lot harder than I imagined, finding that stupid little ball. From a
distance, the natural rolling grasslands of the steppe actually do

look like a golf course. Flying over Mongolia in a plane, an avid golfer might become spastically overcome with excitement, looking at the terrain. But closer inspection tells a different story. A story of weedy, uncontrolled growth. And without any fairway or flagstick as a target, or yardage markers as distance guides, it's more like playing out of the first cut of rough at Carnoustie than the manicured lush fairways of Augusta.

But I'm coping. And I find my second shot after less than a minute of searching. With another "swack," my third shot flies equally as far as my second. I now have reason to be optimistic about my long day ahead. At least I'm golfing well, even if my hands, feet, and back are killing me.

After twenty shots (and only one lost ball), I see a woman and several children collecting dung in the heavy grass. They've got sacks over their shoulders and are using a grasping device that from here looks like the "Grabbit" that I've seen advertised on late-night infomercials. "The indispensable tool for reaching that jar of peanut butter on the top shelf of your kitchen cabinets." I'm not sure if the marketers ever thought of dung-collecting as a potential use for their invention, but it sure seems to me that there's an opportunity here. Dung is still the principal fuel for the countryside home. Mongolians live in gers, and every ger has a stove in the center, where the dung is burned. There is a standard building code for gers that I imagine goes back centuries, because every ger is built in the same manner, with the same internal layout. The dung box is always between the door and the stove, and the stove always sits under the apex of the round, sloped roof. As I watch the people collect the dung, I'm struck by just how self-sufficient the Mongolian people are. They live completely off the land and their livestock. Without this relationship, it would be impossible to survive here. It's a dry, barren landscape, unsuitable for agriculture. But with animals to turn the indigestible (by humans) grass into edible calories in the form of meat and milk, and compact fuel packages in the form of dung, Mongolians have survived, and even thrived, here.

My individual outdoor foray into the wilderness may be impressive to some, but I've got a lightweight multi-fuel cookstove and other high-tech gear. I'm not sure if I could really survive off the land the way these people do. Fortunately, I don't have to, and I can give the dung-pickers a distant-but-friendly wave as I golf past them.

A couple hours later, I'm standing next to a telephone pole, digging into my bag for a handful of raisins. I've lost sight of the river and I haven't spotted the road in over an hour. This is one of those ulcer-inducing moments of indecision. Should I veer to the left in search of the river? or to the right, hoping to cross paths with the main road again? The road and river are my two sure landmarks that will guide me to the next city, and it's a lonely feeling without either of them around. I'm not sure if it's the influence of Mongolian Buddhism or not, but I suddenly and confidently decide on a third alternative, the middle path. I'll just follow these telephone poles. They must continue to Öndörkhaan. Where else could they be going? And even better, telephone poles tend to follow straight lines, so this may actually be the most direct, and therefore smartest, way to go. It's the most confident I've felt in days. My first navigational challenge, albeit a tiny one, and I pass the test.

On my hundredth shot of the day, I see a young man approach me, and then I glimpse a small ger, just a few hundred feet away. He appears to be about fifteen years old, and his face is filled with friendliness and curiosity as he draws nearer. I'm sure my face reflects the same qualities. We stare at each other silently for a moment as if assuming (correctly) that our language difficulties would make it impossible to communicate vocally anyway. Then he motions for me to follow him to the ger. Why not, I think. I could use a rest.

As we approach the ger, I notice that it's a bit smaller than most gers I've seen, and I lay my backpack down on the ground just outside the door. As I duck my head to pass through the short doorframe, a few sets of eyes turn toward me and I say "sain bainuu" to everyone and take a seat on the floor next to the boy who brought me in. Unlike all other gers I've been in before, the floor is dirt, and there is almost no furniture inside. A man sits on the floor silently, a small child crawls around on the dirt pulling on a baby goat, which for some reason is inside the ger, and a woman lies on a simple metal-frame bed with her back to us. The woman, I begin to notice, is moaning and sobbing. No one pays her any attention, and the boy pours me a bowl of tea and offers me some dried curd. Everyone else is quiet.

"Bayarlaa," I say. It's one of the few other Mongolian phrases I know and means "thank you." The man and boy reply stiffly, and then we all turn our gaze to the floor. The woman continues to wail into her pillow, even louder than before. I don't know if she's sick or dying, or has just been beaten, but I'm feeling extremely uncomfortable. All I know is that these people are very poor and very unhappy. I notice that the baby has a rope tied around its ankle to keep it from crawling too close to the stove. Otherwise it's naked, except for the layers of dirt on its small chubby body. I'm keeping my composure, but I'm shocked. I've visited a few Mongolian families in their gers before, but I've never seen one as miserable as this. It makes me realize that even in the subsistence lifestyle of the rural families, there are some who are better off than others. I'm way off the beaten path here, and I'm seeing part of the country that most tourists don't. I'm not sure I need to see any more.

"Well, I guess I ought to be going now," I announce as I stand. "Bayarlaa again." I make my way out the door and swing my backpack up onto my shoulders, forgetting the soreness in my back and the blisters on my feet. I march quickly back to the line of telephone poles and then, with the ger falling out of sight, I drop a golf ball and take a deep breath. Holy shit, that was weird.

I golf twenty more shots, covering about two miles, until I'm sure that I'm unlikely to run into any of those people again. And then I make camp underneath the telephone wires. I'm still disturbed by the family scene that I just witnessed. I wish I could talk to someone now. If I could only tap into those wires above my head and call one of my friends and tell them about my day, how much my body hurts, how strange my encounter was, and how much I'd really love to quit and go home right now.

Instead, I think. I just sit quietly on the grass outside my tent with my face buried in my blister-ridden hands and think. I could call it internal discussion or debate, or whatever. But essentially it's just me sitting for hours by myself. Sitting quietly in the middle of Mongolia, wishing I were somewhere else.

I can walk with pain, grip a golf club with hands full of open, throbbing blisters, and strain my body with every step over the grass. I can continue to torture myself and suffer the physical stress like a beaten dog. That's easy: In fact, I wish all I had to do was take the bodily abuse of this expedition. I'll gladly lose this battle if my body fails me, if I'm not up to the physical challenge. Give me acres of broken glass with nothing but bloody stumps for feet and I'll walk across. But that's not the challenge I face now. No, this obstacle requires much more effort to overcome. This battle is about maintaining control of my mind and resisting the onslaught of depression.

All the signs are here: I've barely eaten anything in the last week; I've spent far too many hours in my sleeping bag, hiding from the world; I've avoided initiating contact with the locals; and I've become uninterested in writing in my journal—or doing anything else creative, for that matter. I sit alone every night in my tent, broken by thoughts of how bad things are.

They're so bad that I wish I couldn't continue on, physically. That something unfortunate could happen to me. That I could break my leg, or get attacked and robbed. Then at least I'd have a reason to quit. I'd have a real, physical, tangible reason to put an end to this idiotic mission. I wouldn't have to anguish over the issue any more, debating whether or not to continue. I'd have clarity.

But nothing bad has happened yet. My appendix hasn't burst, I haven't been bitten by a snake, and I haven't fallen into a crevasse. Yet, I still have hope that any one of these, or any other disastrous event, will set me free. An event to release me from my obligation to go on. A natural disaster would be a good reason to quit. An earthquake, a wildfire, a terrorist attack, anything.

I beg fate for some intervention to justify my failure. Some justification other than the truth. The truth that I want so desperately to hide from the world. The truth that consumes me day and night. The truth that has become so evident, only a lunatic or a cheating golfer could deny it: I'm not tough enough to finish this expedition.

It's day eight. I really believed that things would have gotten better by now. I honestly thought that my muscles would have gotten in better shape to handle the stress, that the blisters would have turned into calluses, and that all the little aches and pains would have disappeared. But they haven't. Just the opposite: they've gotten worse. And the negative thoughts are crowding into my brain with more frequency.

I don't know why I get up every morning and continue golfing toward a distant horizon that I'll never reach. I honestly don't. I wish I could come up with a quote like I've heard other explorers state with such confidence: "I was focused on the achievement of reaching my goal," or "All I could think of was my wonderful children and how much their love kept me going." I don't even have children. And I'm definitely not focused. No, my thoughts are blurred beyond recognition. One minute I'm telling myself that I'll be happy if I just struggle through these early difficult days, and the next minute I'm convinced that it'll never get better and I'll be happiest if I dump all my golf balls and get myself on a plane to a beach in Thailand as soon as possible. And now my motivation and willpower are being eroded by a depression that grows larger by the day.

To add to my troubles, my water supply is running out. Since I left the proximity of the river yesterday to follow this pied-piperish line of telephone poles, I've had no way to fill up the water bottles. The clear plastic one-and-a-half-liter water bottle that I've been refilling since I bought it full in Choibalsan is now empty. That leaves me with only one liter of water in my Yingxing cup. And it's hot today. The cloud cover is gone and the sun is ferociously beating down on me. I've covered about five kilometers so far this morning, and I'm dying to guzzle down that liter of water. But instead, I take tiny sips, letting the moisture roll around my tongue to absorb some of the dust that has risen up into my mouth and nostrils as I've walked. Then I permit the water to flow down into my throat in a pathetic trickle, to be lost forever. It doesn't give me nearly as much pleasure as I hope, rationing my water in this manner. It leaves me with a perpetual feeling of dissatisfaction—and, more often than not, it leaves me still thirsty.

Yet, I dig as deep as I can into my reservoir of self-motivation and continue to hit golf shots, one after the other, knowing that at least the golf will keep my mind away from a growing despon-dency. It's ironic that golf, a game that frustrates and aggravates millions of hackers worldwide, is what keeps me calm now. Knowing how fickle the golf gods are, I hesitate to even mention this, for fear of jinxing myself, but I'm playing extremely well today. Every shot has rocketed off my three-iron, long and straight. Knock on wood. Hitting my fifty-fifth shot of the day, I'm given a reason for optimism. Between the pale yellow sea of grass that stretches out before me and the steel blue of a giant sky, on the linear frontier of the horizon, is a smudge of blinding white. In this place, it can be only one thing: the sharp reflection of a ger, its white canvas roof absorbing not a bit of the sunlight shot in its direction. As I keep my eyes fixed on the object, it separates into two blinding white reflections and I realize that this could be a town.

Letting my backpack fall to the ground with a thud, I withdraw my binoculars for a closer look. It's a string of a dozen gers. I suddenly realize that this could be the little village that marks the end of Hole One. I hold back my optimism in fear of cruel disappointment and check my GPS coordinates and plot them on my map. My finger moves along the map until it rests over the tiny black typeface that reads "Tosontsengel." This village has fewer than forty residents, lacks a post office and town hall, and in any other country would not warrant its own little black dot on a map. It could be called a one-horse town, except here in Mongolia where horses outnumber people the minimum number of horses needed to escape small-town status is much higher. Here, a twenty-horse town is about as small as it gets. But what it lacks in size, it makes up for in importance. In my world, this place is on a par with New York or London, for this town represents a milestone—the conclusion to the first hole of my cross-country course.

I'm alerted to the fact that I'm only a few steps away from the road when I hear a van approaching me from behind, raising a great cloud of dust in its wake. As it darts past me, I raise my hand and wave. I'm inspired to be friendly and cheerful with the sudden turn of events.

The van slams on its brakes, and then starts to reverse toward me. Uh-oh. What did I do now? I'm more afraid of having to explain myself in broken Mongolian than anything else, though I wouldn't blame a passing vehicle for expressing some curiosity in me. It's not every day that the locals see a foreigner with a backpack and a golf club walking alone in this end of the country, far from any tourist sights. The driver's window rolls down and as the van stops at my side, I recognize the man. Well, whaddya know?

It's the same van driver that Alain and I had from Ulaan Baatar to Choibalsan. The guy who I almost got into a fight with. This is certainly an unlikely occurrence, running into someone I know out here in the middle of nowhere. He reaches his arm out the window to shake my hand and starts talking excitedly in Mongolian.

"Hey! Yeah, I remember you," I offer, cutting him off in mid-sentence. "Well, here I am, all the way from Choibalsan." At the mention of the word Choibalsan, he turns his head back to several passengers and says, "See, I told you this was the guy. This crazy bastard actually walked here all the way from Choibalsan, hitting a little white ball!" I guess that's what he said because, as he finishes, all the passengers turn their heads back to me and give me the kind of look you'd give if you just saw an albino moose walk through your backyard and tell you he was on his way to Mexico to get a tan.

The driver motions toward the back seat to ask me if I want a ride into the town. "No, thanks, I'll walk and meet you there," I say as I make two of my fingers into little legs to indicate a walking movement. We both point ahead to the town and nod in agreement.

The van grinds into gear and pulls ahead as the faces in the windows stay glued in my direction. I can't get the smile off my face as the dust cloud once again billows up to obscure the view of the passengers from the back windows.

I don't bother to search any more for my previous shot and instead drop a ball in the vicinity of where I think it should be. I've lost count of my steps, and my golf rhythm has been completely interrupted. But I don't care. After days alone in a near-depression, I now feel like I have a friend.

My fifth shot after the encounter sails across a small dry creekbed and lands in the middle of the sandy road that forms Tosontsengel's main street. Actually, its only street. And maybe that's even being too generous. This dirt track isn't unique to this town, but is part of the main east—west highway of Mongolia, linking all the regional capitals. The road is called the Millennium Highway. Or at least that's what I was told by an Australian woman in UB when I showed her a map of my route.

"Oh, so you're golfing along the Millennium Highway then," she mentioned in a knowing tone. "Yeah, exactly," I replied. "You know, most of the way I'll be sort of close to the highway." I had no idea what I was talking about; but I felt as if I should be more of an authority on Mongolian affairs, so I bluffed my way through.

The highway, I learned later, is an ambitious initiative by the Mongolian government to construct an asphalt-paved road from one end of the country to the other (coincidentally with roughly the same starting and finishing points as my golf journey). This is indeed ambitious when you consider that the entire country of Mongolia has only seven hundred miles of paved highways. To put this in perspective, consider that Rhode Island's state highway system consists of 1,100 miles of paved roads and you could fit 390 Rhode Islands into the borders of Mongolia.

So the country must be filled with railroad tracks then, you're thinking.

Absolutely not. There is only one main set of tracks in Mongolia; it branches off the trans-Siberian line near Lake Baikal and shoots down to China, passing through Ulaan Baatar on the way. There's also a rail link off of this line to the city of Erdenet in the north, but this line only exists because of the enormous copper mine in Erdenet and the heavy investment that the Soviet Union made to gain access to the lode of ore. So, as you see, this is a country with an almost nonexistent transportation infrastructure, and that's clearly a hindrance to the development of the economy.

Of course, the real beauty of the Millennium Highway project is that Mongolia plans to build it with other governments' money, or at least part of it. A large portion of the road construction costs so far has come from Japanese foreign aid and Asia Development Bank loans. It's as if the Mongolians are saying to the rest of the developed world: "If you want to sell cars here, then you pay for the roads." But it'll be a long time before the road is finished. I thought originally that it was called the Millennium Highway because it was scheduled for completion in the year 2000. But now I'm realizing that at the current construction pace, they'll be more likely to finish in about a thousand years, maintaining the accuracy of the road's title. But my immediate concern is finishing this hole.

With one more swing, my ball rolls across the compacted dirt and in front of a group of children who look up at me for a moment, trying to gauge my demeanor, and then chase the ball down and scoop it up, yelling and running after one another. I guess that'll be the final shot for this hole, and the kids will keep the souvenir.

The end of hole one. A milestone. At this moment, I am exactly one-eighteenth of the way across the country. I think about this for a moment and suddenly realize with some chagrin that the fraction *one-eighteenth* feels quite minuscule, so I convert it to a decimal number. My journey is officially 5.6 percent complete. This doesn't feel much better. For all I've been through, I need a reward better than this. Eleven percent. Yes, I think 11 percent of the way through the first *nine* holes is how I'll measure this moment. This is much more satisfying. I can be pleased now as I march past the children and a few other adults who glare at me curiously.

"Sain bainuu!" I say, lifting my hand in a wave to all the onlookers. "Sain bainuu," they all reply and then return to their business, satisfied that I'm not all that strange if I can at least say hello in their language. I continue all the way through town to the last ger, where the van is parked. The driver stands outside and beckons me to enter the low wood-framed doorway into the ger. Ducking my head and stepping carefully onto the wooden floor (among many superstitions and customs that the Mongolians follow is the practice of never stepping on the door sill), I follow the gestures of a middle-aged man toward an empty seat on a bed. It feels great to sit down. This ger functions as a roadside café, and the old woman who resides here is frantically preparing food for the fifteen of us who just arrived. Her incessant fussing over our meals and positive disposition instantly endear her to me, and I decide to call her Granny.

"Are you hungry?" My eyes shoot up instantly to the source of these words spoken in English. "Yes, I'm very hungry," I reply to a young Mongolian woman seated at a wooden table to my right. She repeats this in Mongolian to Granny. Wow, a translator! I introduce myself and learn that her name is Oyuna. Sensing that everyone is curious about me, she takes the initiative to ask me several questions. "Where are you from? How old are you? Are you married? Where are you going?" She translates my answers to the enraptured audience until the man sitting next to me, who has been continually touching my arm while waiting his turn, finally bursts out in a question of his own. I wait for the translation as the man and I look at each other. "Do you like vodka?"

If there were a collection of vodkas of the world, ranked by quality, then Mongolia's contributions would do a fine job of filling in the bottom of the list. I know this because I've tried many.

During my visit to this country in 2001, I entered a shop with my traveling companion, Daniel, with the goal of picking up a couple bottles for the road before venturing out into the countryside. "Let's get something good," I said. His quick reply evidently revealed that he, too, had sampled enough "bad" vodka to warrant an additional expenditure for "something good." Much to our surprise, the most expensive bottle carried a price of four dollars, with dozens of brands in the one- to two-dollar range. We splurged for the four-dollar bottle, and later received the satisfaction of knowing that we'd paid a little extra for a chug-and-wince drinking experience and subsequent head-splitting hangover. There is little justification for using the words *good* and *Mongolian vodka* in the same sentence.

But despite the opinions of most foreigners as to the quality of the vodka in their country, Mongolians love the stuff. I presume that this has something to do with the past eighty years of close relationships with Russian expatriates working and living here. It takes only the slightest pretense of a special occasion for them to crack open a bottle. And this was no exception; so when I replied enthusiastically: "Yeah, I like vodka," he motioned with authority to our hostess, who promptly withdrew a bottle from a small cabinet.

I'm not quite sure why I replied so emphatically. Perhaps I was so stricken with happiness to be with people again that I wanted to appear as cooperative as possible, so as not to lose their friendship. Or perhaps after eight days of hell, I just really needed a drink.

"My name is Uul," the man says as he twists the cap on the vodka bottle. *Uul* means "mountain" in Mongolian, and the name more accurately describes his width than his height. "André," I reply, pointing to myself rather foolishly, as if he'd think I was referring to someone else.

"Andrei?! *Ti govoresh po-russki?*" I only understand enough Russian to know that I don't speak it well, and I reply with a definitive *"Nyet."* I think this only encourages him to try out some more Russian on me, and, as he hands me a cup of vodka, he laughs and says *"Droga!"* I remember from my elementary Russian class sixteen years ago that this means "friend."

"Droga!" I say, raising the glass and shooting it straight back. It's one of the two-dollar bottles that we're drinking, and I immediately realize that maybe I shouldn't have blessed the idea of vodka consumption so wholeheartedly.

I'm given an enormous plate of noodles and mutton, with a few pieces of onion making a token appearance. This food looks fantastic. After nothing but bland vegetarian fare for the past week, the chunks of meat, at least half of which are fat (and even the white fat is coated with oil from the stir-fry), look especially mouth-watering.

Uul and I continue to chat throughout our meal, with the help of Oyuna's translations. I learn that he is the boss of the transport company that arranges these vans to and from Ulaan Baatar. I explain in more detail the nature of my expedition, and he remains impressed.

"*Naiz, droga, hao peng* you," he declares in Mongolian, Russian, and Chinese as he hands me another glass of vodka.

"Friend!" I add in English.

"Fren!" he repeats, delighted with the idea of adding a fourth language to his repertoire.

We continue with the naiz-droga-friend routine until the bottle is empty. "You don't have to pay for your food," he makes clear and directs a second helping of noodles onto my plate. "I have CNN in my apartment in Ulaan Baatar. You can mention my name, Uul, when you're on television." It seems like a fair deal to me, and I dig into my second helping of *tsuivan*, the noodle-and-mutton dish. Then another bottle of vodka appears.

I was somewhat relieved when the first bottle was finished. Some of the other men in the ger had taken a few sips, but Uul and I had done most of the heavy lifting. Now, the prospect of having to finish a second bottle had me frightened. The novelty of a noontime drink in celebration of finishing the first hole had worn off, and enthusiasm turned into dread. I know that the crackle of a cap being turned on a vodka bottle in Mongolia means that no one goes anywhere until the bottle is finished. But like a paralyzed locomotive engineer watching two trains on the same track, I could do nothing to stop the impending disaster.

An hour later, Oyuna leans toward me and says: "You should rest here for a while. The sun is too hot out there."

"No, I'll be fine," I begin, somewhat slurred. "Well, all right," I continue, "maybe a little rest." I say good-bye to Uul and the rest of the crowd as they file out the door and back into the van.

"He says he'll probably see a lot more of you," says Oyuna, pointing to the van driver. "He drives this road every other day."

"Tell him if he does, then to stop and give me some water," I reply.

With a final wave to Uul and the van driver, I settle back down onto the bed and close my eyes. The first hole is now complete.

Day eleven. It's the hottest day of the expedition so far. At nine o'clock in the morning, I can already feel the sweat start to form in little beads under my crusty T-shirt as I walk away from the row of gers to take a leak. The sweat on my skin has the faint odor of vodka, and I should probably have a worse hangover than I do, but the fifteen hours of sleep I just had has mitigated the aftereffects of my vodka binge quite well.

Turning my face back to the sun and walking toward the gers, I sidestep piles of dung that are slowly drying into solid cakes of fuel to be used throughout the year, and I pass by an oxcart with a broken axle. The heat of the day will surely be oppressing, but there

is no charm in this dusty ramshackle town to lure me into pro-
longing my stay. I open the door to Granny's ger and step inside.

She already has a fire roaring inside the black sheet-metal stove,
and she's stirring a pan of milk tea with a large metal ladle. In a
fluid, cyclic motion that exhibits years of experience with this routine, she lifts a ladle of the milky broth high in the air and pours it
slowly back into the round woklike pan, repeating this procedure
continuously and only stopping briefly to toss in a handful of salt. I
don't know if she's aerating, mixing, or cooling the stuff, but I do
know that it's mesmerizing to watch, especially in my groggy,
mildly hung-over state of consciousness.

My trance is broken when the door swings open and a shaft of
sunlight beams across my face. Squinting, I watch the right foot of
a man dressed in heavy leather boots step across the threshold. "Sain
bainuu?" I offer confidently.

"Sain, sain bainuu," he replies, the last part of his speech trailing
off into an inaudible exhalation of breath as he bends down and
grabs a tiny wooden stool, plunks it down next to me and then settles his body onto it. We exchange a few questions and answers as
best as we can over the next ten minutes, and I figure out that he's
the son of the old woman in the ger. I figure this out, clever bastard
that I am, because as he points to the family photo album, he's in
most of the pictures at varying ages, and so is Granny. The photo
album is not so much an album per se, but a collection of snapshots
and Polaroids tucked and taped around a rectangular mirror,

which rests on a dresser that is painted orange and blue in Tibetan style. There are about forty photos in all, most showing family members in Ulaan Baatar or other cities, posing in front of monuments or buildings. A few pictures, which appear to be very old, show a man standing in Red Square and other locations around Moscow.

After the family history presentation, the man jumps up and opens the door and reaches up to the roof of the ger. He brings a plastic bag inside and opens it to reveal what looks to me to be a partial leg of mutton. I can't tell if it's been smoked or boiled, but it's a ghastly looking piece of meat. The man gleefully withdraws his knife and slices off a slab of fat with a few strips of brown meat at its edges. He places the slab into the open palm of my hand and encourages me to have a bite.

"Holy crap! Am I really expected to eat this?" I silently ponder. This gigantic mass of calorie-laden lard would certainly make any supermodel faint, or would at least knock her down if you flopped it against the side of her head. I don't think I've ever eaten this much fat at one time before (it's the equivalent of an entire stick of butter), but I'm sure that I'll easily burn off the calories, so I take a big bite. The cold fat squeezes around my teeth as I try to keep from gagging on the slightly rancid taste. Luckily, Granny's salty milky tea has been served and I can quickly wash down the unchewable bits.

Calories are currency in this country where fickle weather or sick livestock can easily plunge a family toward starvation. Walking across the land carrying a heavy load on my back, I realize intimately the importance of maintaining enough energy for sustainability. The chunk of fat this man has given me is a wad of cash in caloric terms, and I'd be callous not to appreciate his generosity. Against the overwhelming reluctance of my senses to put my mouth anywhere near the blobby, stinking morsel, I push on to the last bite, desperately wishing I had some Dijon mustard to mask the taste and texture.

The glorious cuisine aside, there isn't much reason for me to linger; I should get going. I say my farewells to the mother and son and prepare myself to meet the day, and the start of hole two. When any golfer finishes a hole, they pick up their ball, proceed to the next hole, and tee up the ball. Although it's on a slightly larger scale, my eighteen holes of golf across Mongolia are following the same concept.

A hundred paces to the west of Granny's ger, I drop my pack and pull out a new golf ball and a white tee. I've hit shots off dozens of species of grass and weeds in the past ten days, but nothing compares to whacking the ball when it's propped up perfectly on a wooden tee. I begin to get excited again as my thumb pushes the little tee into the dirt. Mutton fat and salty tea aside, this adventure is about golf. I take my first swing of the day.

My rejuvenated enthusiasm lasts about an hour and a half. Perhaps this is how long it took for the mutton-fat calories to burn off. Now the little town is out of sight and I'm completely alone, heading off into a field of grass that stretches farther than I can see.

My feet are sending bolts of pain up through my body every time I put pressure on my blister-ridden soles, my back is aching, and I'm getting cooked in the midday sun. I'm slowly returning to the hell that I had avoided for nearly twenty-four hours.

I've got to find a way to distract myself or I'll drive myself crazy dwelling on my miserable circumstances and the stupidity of this whole expedition.

Miraculously, this distraction comes as I rise from my short rest on the ground and prepare to hit another shot—I can't remember my score. I know it's either twenty-seven or twenty-six but I can't decide if I hit the twenty-seventh or if I was just thinking about it before I decided to rest. One might think that it really doesn't matter in the whole scheme of things if I get the score wrong, all alone out here in the middle of the wilderness. But it does to me. What's the point of keeping score if I can't keep it properly? I'm not an obsessive maniac about proper scorekeeping on the golf course, but it seems to have increased in importance now, here in Mongolia.

In that Tom Hanks movie where he's a castaway on an uninhabited island for years, he holds on to one FedEx package that's washed ashore, and keeps it unopened, in the hope that some day he'll get off the island and deliver it. I know it's not as drastic for me, but my scorekeeping is my FedEx package. It provides some structure to my otherwise miserable day; and if I can't do that right, then there's no reason to go on at all.

I'm calling it "twenty-seven." It might be only twenty-six, but I recognize that most golfers tend to underestimate their score rather than overestimate it and this is most likely true now. I could contemplate the motives, conscious or subconscious, behind this tendency, but suspect scorekeeping is an area of discussion I'd rather avoid. Golf is a gentleman's game, after all. So it's shot number twenty-eight coming up. And that's when I think of Herbert Hoover.

Though vacuum cleaners come to mind faster than presidents when the name Hoover is mentioned, Herbert was in fact elected president of the United States in 1928. It's not a particularly well-known presidency, but a history teacher somewhere will be proud to know that I associate the number twenty-eight with 1928 and Herbert Hoover. He was president during the great stock market crash of 1929, and that event comes to mind as I prepare to hit my twenty-ninth shot of the day. I never knew history lessons would ever be as useful as they are now. Pondering the events of each year in the twentieth century is a welcome distraction from my increasingly negative thoughts about my physical suffering.

It also becomes too difficult a challenge to maintain, and by the time I reach thirty-one shots, I'm thinking about sports. The basketball player—Cedric Maxwell, to be more precise—as he donned the number 31 on his uniform for the Boston Celtics more than twenty years ago. I was a big fan of the four professional sports teams in Boston when I was growing up: the Red Sox, Celtics, Bruins, and Patriots. Such a big fan that I can remember the uniform numbers of many of the most obscure players from my childhood era. Gary Allenson, a backup catcher for the Red Sox from 1979 to 1984, wore number 39. In the early 1980s, Gerald Henderson of the Celtics wore number 43, while another guard for the same team, Danny Ainge, wore number 44. Tim Fox, a safety for the Patriots from 1976 to 1981, wore number 48.

Between my tenuous grasp of twentieth-century history, uniform numbers of my sports idols as a child, and personal lucky numbers, birthdays, and graduations, I can associate nearly every two-digit number with some event or person, an associative strategy that serves as a mind-occupying pacifier as I count my daily golf shots up to a hundred, and then start all over again. This strategy works so well that I'll continue using it on every day of the expedition to come.

Just after I think of Carl Yastrzemski batting his way to the Triple Crown (going 23 for 44 in the last two weeks of the season) and leading the Red Sox to a heart-wrenching loss in the World Series (that was in 1967, for the non-sports-minded), the population of my lonely world increases to two, as I spot a man on horseback riding toward me. He's a middle-aged man with a large red burn mark covering half his face, and he looks a bit intimidating from a distance.

After a silent pause, he motions to a ger on the adjacent hill, and I presume that he's inviting me to his home. To his delight, I take one more shot and send the ball flying up the hill toward his home.

His stern demeanor has loosened up a bit after witnessing what may have been the first three-iron shot he's ever seen. Before turning my attention to the limited conversation I'll have with my new acquaintance, I pause to make a mental note of my score and think of 1968 and the assassination of Robert F. Kennedy.

There's a crowd outside the man's ger. At least a dozen people are busily working, and all of them stop to have a look at me. Several join me and the older man as we walk inside the ger. It's cool and shady inside. This is the first opportunity I've had all day to get some relief from the pounding heat of the sun. I'm offered a bowl of salty milky tea.

I could easily rattle off a list of cold refreshing beverages that would satisfy my parched throat and growing thirst, with just plain water being somewhere near the top of the list. But hot Mongolian tea? It's the last thing I would want. Still, I sip it sparingly out of politeness. At least it's useful in washing down the dried curd that I've been given. It's true that beggars can't be choosers, as the proverb says; but, Christ, it would be nice to have something cold at least!

Despite my perturbation at the choice of beverages I was offered, I'm pretty happy at having a chance to rest in the shade and have some human contact, and I show my appreciation of their hospitality by engaging them in a conversation, with the help of my Mongolian phrase book.

"How are the livestock?" I ask stutteringly. It takes a second for them to realize what I'm trying to say before three of them all try to speak at the same time to answer my question. I mostly just nod my head and smile at their responses. One man in his early twenties leans against me and takes my phrase book. He flips through the pages until finally stopping and then pointing to a phrase confidently, as if he knew all along that that was where he'd find the exact phrase he was looking for. I glance down at his index finger, the skin noticeably darkened from the sun and the fingernail dirty and unmanicured. The English phrase it points to is "arable land."

"Uh-huh, arable land. Yes, I see." Nodding my head several times, I respond positively. I can't find any other phrase on the page that would keep the conversation going forward in any kind of logical progression, so I have another sip of my tea. A young boy of about ten says something to the others, and then we all stand up and go outside. I hadn't noticed it on the way in, but there's a fence made of wood lattice with about thirty sheep inside just behind the ger. Two men are taking the sheep one by one and dragging them onto a wooden platform and tying up their back legs. Then two women and the other adult man join in the activity. They're shearing the sheep.

I had never actually witnessed sheep-shearing before, and certainly not with old-fashioned manual shears. It's a remarkable operation. They've herded the sheep on horseback, corralled them into a pen, and now are cutting them out one by one, shearing them, and then letting them go back to the steppe. The whole family is taking part in this: young and old, boys and girls. I get in for a close look,

and a woman laughs as she effortlessly snips and cuts away the wool
before handing me the giant scissors, as if to say "Here, you try." So
I do. I've got no clue what I'm doing, but I clip enough wool to
make a respectable pile. Mostly, I'm relieved not to have a stream of
blood running down the poor sheep's belly, but I also realize that I
should be moving on and making some more progress today. The
family seems sad to see me go, as if they're saying good-bye to some
long-lost cousin who they might not see again for a long time. The
mother of the family gives me a plastic bag filled with dried curd
and a creamy substance that looks like runny scrambled eggs. I'm
not sure if I'll enjoy eating these Mongolian dairy delicacies, but I
accept the offer graciously and wave good-bye to the whole clan.

Retreating down the hill to the spot where my sixty-eighth shot
landed, I once again resume my current raison d'être, hitting golf
balls across this foreign land. I hit shot number sixty-nine, lug the
heavy backpack up onto my shoulders, and begin the slow method-
ical trudge to the west. A well-worn pair of wheel ruts leads off
through the valley, and I'm confident that this is the main road that
will lead me to the end of hole two. One step at a time, I move
across the land, trying to ignore the pain and focus on maintaining
a steady rate of progress.

In the late afternoon, my body tells me that it's time to quit. I've
hit 124 shots and I've spent the better part of nine hours under the
direct gaze of the sun. I've got just enough energy left to set up my
tent and to search for water. My water bottles are empty, and the

river has meandered out of sight and away from the road over the last few miles, so I'm taking a leap of faith in assuming that it's within a reasonable walking distance.

Leaving all my possessions behind in my tent, I set off with my water filter and two bottles toward a line of shrubs and low trees that are easily recognizable on the otherwise grass-covered terrain. I soon learn an important lesson that I will continuously relearn throughout my trip—on the flat featureless steppe, distances are easy to misjudge. What looks like a half mile might actually be two miles. This looks to be the case now. Twenty minutes into my river search, I realize my error in judgment: I'm not even halfway to the bushy vegetation that I saw from my tent. As I silently curse this damned but self-inflicted predicament, I notice three figures approaching me on horseback. I immediately think of all my valuables, including my passport and all my money, lying there unattended in my tent. I had thought this to be a desolate and uninhabited portion of the countryside; but on second thought, I'm sure my tent and even my own silhouette are easily visible from a long distance. The riders continue to move quickly toward me.

The three horses slow to a walk, bringing their human passengers within speaking distance. They are three boys aged fourteen to nineteen, and I break the silence by saying hello. They return my salutation and ask me a question that I can't understand. I assume they're asking me what the hell I'm doing here, so I try to ask how far it is to the river.

"Kherlen Gol *khana baina ve?*" I venture.

The oldest boy points straight ahead as the other two begin to rapidly converse with each other. The oldest again takes on the role as translator and holds up the reins of his horse as if he's offering them to me.

"Oh, no, I couldn't possibly . . . ," I begin to mumble. But before I know it, he's off his horse and handing me the leather reins and jumping up onto the horse of the smallest of his companions. "Come on, let's go. We'll all go together," they enthusiastically offer. Well, what the hell, it beats walking. I plant my left foot onto a metal stirrup and swing myself up onto the horse and into the small wooden saddle.

A note about saddles. There are lots of different types of saddles to be found all around the world. Equestrians might easily debate the various shapes and sizes and the advantages of the English saddle versus the common Western saddle, for example. But never have I heard anyone discussing the merits of the Mongolian saddle—or even the existence of it, for that matter. Which is weird, because the Mongolians conquered half the world on horseback and are known for being exceptional horsemen. One might expect that they would have developed some sort of highly advanced saddle by now. But that's not the case. Mongolians use wooden saddles.

These saddles, as one would expect, are not easy on the backside. And as if the lack of cushioning wasn't bad enough, the narrow saddle curves sharply up in the front and back to snugly wedge in the rider's crotch. It's damn close to being a torture device, and I understand why most Mongolian men stand up in the stirrups as they ride. But on the positive side, as I ride with my three new companions toward the river, at least it's my groin that aches instead of my feet.

I learn that the three boys are brothers and their names are Bataa, Boldoo, and Bogii. (To my delight I learn that Bogii, pronounced like bogey, really is a male name in Mongolia.) We dismount at the river after a fifteen-minute ride and I limp down to the riverbank with my water filter, eager to display my sophisticated camping technology. I've been impressed with my new filter/purifier up to this point. It takes the churning, muddy water of the Kherlen River and turns it into perfectly clear, potable fluid. But this is where my lack of experience as an outdoorsman catches up with me. The filter is clogged.

It makes perfect sense to me now that I never should have expected the miraculous cleansing technology to have continued forever. I even remember reading in the owner's manual something about using a prefilter in cases where the source water is extremely turbid. Glancing at the chocolate-colored watercourse in front of me, I suspect this is exactly the type of high turbidity that they were referring to.

The three boys seem eager to help with my filter, but I assure them that I've got it under control, and I reconfigure the device for the "backwashing" process. Fifteen minutes of laborious struggle soon follow. I've slipped down the muddy riverbank a few times, and the filler tube on my filter has popped off twice, soaking the front of my shirt in the process, but I've succeeded in getting two liters of clean water. In the meantime, the two eldest boys have been sitting on the grass smoking Monte Carlo brand cigarettes while the horses have steadily munched away on the lush vegetation. I feel like a dickhead. I come from a country where we think we have advanced learning and technology, and yet I don't know the slightest thing about real survival out here in the wilderness. The fragility of my water filter shows just how fragile my own existence and survival out here really are. And I'm just here as a tourist for the summer. These people live here year-round, through the forty-below temperatures of the harsh winter and the gale-force winds of the springtime dust storms. Without my high-tech solutions, I'd die pretty quickly out here. They make it look easy. Even now, these three boys in front of me are laughing and having a good time. Maybe they're laughing at me, but I don't care. I like their attitude. Tossing the filled water bottle down on the ground, I sit down next to them and take one of the Monte Carlo smokes that Boldoo offers me.

We chat for a while before jumping back up onto the horses. They've invited me to their family's ger, and I've accepted the offer. I know that I probably wouldn't have had the energy to bother with cooking any dinner for myself, so this is a great opportunity to enjoy some company and get a hot meal.

The boys are talkative and easygoing, and I understand why when I meet their mother, a round-faced jolly woman of nonstop busyness, and their father, a man with a quick and easy smile that implies that he's happy with the way life is going. It's easy to feel comfortable here.

The big pot of mutton-and-noodle soup that sits over the stove in the middle of their ger makes it even easier. I'm slowly catching on to this Mongolian cuisine and, halfway through my second bowl of soup, I no longer wish I had a bottle of Tabasco sauce with me. I'm becoming conscious of the different aftertastes of the boiled mutton itself and the dissolved mutton grease that floats on the surface of the bowl. It's a subtle variance in flavor, like the way boiled potatoes and baked potatoes taste slightly different, or how soft-boiled and hard-boiled eggs differ in taste and texture. It's a simple cuisine here, but one where the adventurous and open-minded diner could still learn a few lessons on how to tickle the taste buds.

But eventually, the topic of conversation turns to the item that this family finds most curious—my golf club. I try hard to explain, with the help of my piss-poor phrase book, exactly what I'm doing; but in the end, it's when I make a little walking man out of my two fingers and say "Ulaan Baatar" that they finally get it. I'm walking to Ulaan Baatar and playing golf along the way. They seem so distressed, or maybe impressed (I can't tell), by this project of mine that I don't have the heart to explain that I'm actually going all the way across the country to Khovd. Instead, we head outside for an impromptu round of mini-golf.

After an hour of teaching the three boys how to grip the club properly and eventually how to chip properly (not easy with a three-iron), Bogii suddenly appears with a soccer ball, and now a game of soccer is under way. The youthful enthusiasm of these guys is so contagious that I ignore the blisters on my feet and join in the game. I've been mired in misery so much over the past week that I can't resist this opportunity to just have fun.

Exhausted, we retire to the ger just as the sun sets. On the way back, we stop where the boys had tied up the horses in back of their home. There's a simple horse-hitching contraption behind the ger with two poles driven into the ground and a rope tied between them so that it looks like a cross between a volleyball net and a clothesline. Boldoo leads me over to one of the horses and shows me how to unbridle it and take off the reins and saddle. Then he hobbles the horse by tying three of its legs together with leather straps so that the horse can't take a full stride very easily, like a chain-gang prisoner. Then he points to the second horse and asks me to do it. I'm nervous, but with Boldoo's calm instruction and a newfound sense of confidence in myself, I succeed in doing everything correctly. I realize that this is his way of saying "thanks for showing me how to play golf, now I'll show you how to do something you've never done before." Suddenly he seems much more mature to me than his boyish face would suggest. This kid's going to go far in life.

I set up my tent about twenty feet to the west of the ger and prepare to crawl inside. A blood-red full moon has risen and the stars are beginning to spackle the midnight blue sky with dots of light. It's a perfect night, to end an incredible day.

In my sleeping bag, I feel my body move quickly toward the immobile and unconscious state of existence that it desperately needs. But I allow myself a moment of conscious reflection first. Today, I shared the hospitality of two Mongolian families. I sheared sheep and hobbled a horse for the first time in my life. I taught the game of golf to people who had never seen it before. I laughed and joked and communicated with people who didn't speak the same language as me. And most important, I felt at home in Mongolia.

These are the experiences that I had set out to gain. This is why I've endured so much pain and pushed myself to carry on without question. For the very first time on this expedition, I feel like I have a reason to continue.

If necessity is the mother of invention,

then resourcefulness is the father.

—Beulah Louise Henry, U.S. inventor

ndré! What the hell are you doing here?"

"It's a long story, but I came back to make a few modifications."

"Oh shit, I can't believe this! What do you mean? What kind of modifications?"

"I need a cart."

Alain combines the feelings of sympathy, surprise, and skepticism into one look. But overall, I can tell he's happy to see me. I'm sitting in one of Ulaan Baatar's newest Internet cafés, which are popping up all over the city. I'm updating my Web site with my scores and other statistics, as well as progress reports. I've also sent e-mail to all my close friends and family members to let them know I'm alive.

"You've lost some weight, man! When did you get back?"

"Late last night. I got a ride from these people who saw me near Öndörkhaan. They had this truckload of sheep and goats. It was really weird."

Randomly bizarre might be a more accurate description of my encounter with George and the others. I was midway through Hole Three yesterday, searching for one of my nice Callaway golf balls, when a Russian Forgon minivan, along with a truck-and-trailer full of goats and sheep, pulled off the road and stopped next to me. George approached me first. A short, stocky Mongolian man with a thick black moustache, George would be classified by many as a simple man. I could quickly tell that he wasn't the sort of man who would ever win the Nobel Prize, but he certainly knew how to handle goats and sheep, and he had this exact responsibility for the truckload and trailer-load of livestock that he was accompanying. George and I hit it off right away. His English vocabulary was no better than my Mongolian, but his ever-present smile and deliberate hand gestures made him easy to talk to.

Probably in his mid-thirties, George had no trouble jumping up onto the bed of the truck that contained about forty sheep and goats crammed tightly together. He manhandled the animals effortlessly, lifting them by their horns and repositioning them side by side in their close quarters. Then he did the same in the eight-wheel trailer that was connected to the truck by a long towbar. An equal amount of sorting and repositioning needed to be done. Then, jumping down, he returned to slap me on the back and engage me in conversation.

"*Yamar uls?*" he asks, requesting my country of origin.

"America."

"America *sain!*" George nods his head and gives me a thumbs-up sign, confirming his statement that America is good.

I notice three women exit the Forgon and walk off into the grass on the opposite side of the van from George and me. They're obviously heading to the ladies' room. Two men also get out of the van, and they approach me to see what I'm doing and also to see how I'm dealing with George.

"America," he informs the others and then turns to me with a serious face. "Whiskey?"

"Whiskey sain," I say, using the same sentence construction that he just used for me. Then I give him the thumbs-up sign as well.

"Ha ha ha ha ha ha!" George slaps his thigh uncontrollably. I have no clue why he's laughing but upon reflection I do find the randomness of it all to be quite amusing. In fact, the situation is so bizarre that I suddenly feel like I could actually use a shot of whiskey, so I point to George and ask, "You, whiskey?"

"You, whiskey," he replies.

"No, you whiskey?" I repeat.

"Ha ha ha ha ha ha! America sain, whiskey sain!" Something's been lost in the translation and I get the feeling that this could go on a long time.

The other two guys grow impatient with the Laurel and Hardy routine, and they engage me with a few questions. I do my best to explain my expedition, but they understand best when I make the little walking motion with my two fingers again and say Ulaan Baatar. By now, the women have returned, and the men explain to them that I'm walking to Ulaan Baatar. They all sternly express their disapproval at such an endeavor and shake their heads disbelievingly.

Their disbelief triggers my own skepticism about the sanity of this expedition. And I haven't even told them about the golf part of it yet, or the fact that I'm actually walking all the way to Khovd, another eighteen hundred kilometers! They're right, this is crazy. And when they point to the open door of the van and an empty seat, and explain that they're also going to Ulaan Baatar, it's just too good an offer to turn down. I take about half a second to think about it before picking up my fifty-pound backpack and saying "Let's go!"

The next thing I know, I'm bouncing along in the back of a Forgon van with my legs stretched out, chatting to five Mongolians about myself and my expedition using very basic Mongolian. I learn that they have all come from Choibalsan this morning and that the three women are just catching a lift to the capital while the three men are taking the sheep and goats somewhere to sell them. Peering out the back window, I can see the outline of George's stout forearms on the steering wheel of the truck. I make a comment in Mongolian about George being a nice guy. The men laugh and shake their heads. "George Bush," one of them says and laughs, obviously thinking this is funny but probably having no idea why I'm doubled over in laughter at the thought of this comparison.

"We didn't arrive until eleven last night," I continue explaining to Alain. "It was an excruciatingly slow ride. We stopped about every hour and George would jump into the back of the truck and trailer every time to straighten out the sheep. And every time, he would come to me and mumble an incoherent sentence that contained the words *America* and *whiskey* before descending into laughter."

"So what are you going to do now?" Alain asks.

"Well, like I said, I need a cart. You know those really nice baby strollers with the three huge wheels? I need one of those, or something like that. My fucking backpack is just way too heavy. I can't carry it any more."

Alain shoots me one of those "I told you so" glances. "You did pretty well to make it this far," he replies, generously.

"Yeah, but I'm serious, I couldn't have made it one more day. You should see the blisters on my feet. And I was running out of water every day and there was no way that I could carry more. I had to give away a bunch of my food."

I'm referring to the morning when I left the family of Boldoo, Bataa, and Bogii. They were so generous to me that I wanted to give something back, so I donated a two-pound bag of rice, a pound of pasta, and the bag of dried curd and creamy stuff that I had gotten from the sheep-shearing family. Although my secondary motive was to lighten my load a bit and it almost felt like they were doing me a favor by accepting these things, I'm sure they appreciated the gifts.

"What have you been eating?"

"Not much, really. Mostly just raisins and peanuts during the day. In the mornings I was having a couple packets of the MacCereal."

"And that was it? No wonder you lost weight."

"Well, it didn't make any sense to make soup or rice or pasta, because they used up so much water. As it was, I had to ration out every sip." I don't even bother telling him about the psychological stress of running out of water nearly every day. But I do relate the story of how I cooked pasta one night and then drank the milky, starch-filled water that I had cooked it in.

"It was probably full of nutrition, anyway," Alain points out.

"Yeah, but it tasted like shit. You don't understand."

What he could never understand is how depressing it was to be forced to drink that cloudy pasta water. To have the constant worry of running out of water on top of constantly having an unquench-able thirst. How desperate I felt and how much internal strength it took for me to carry on as long as I did. He would never be able to understand any of that.

All these feelings are rekindled again as Alain recounts how he has spent the past two weeks. The joy of wondrous experiences comes through his voice as he tells his stories, and this joy gets silently contrasted with the miserable existence that I've led during that same time.

"From Choibalsan, I stopped for one night in Öndörkhaan and then came directly back to UB," he relates. "When I got back to the guest house, there was an Australian couple and a Swedish couple who were about to head off to the countryside in a van. I basically sat down with them and told them where we should go and then we just went. It was awesome." He recounts his awe of traveling up to Lake Hövsgöl and various other beautiful regions of Mongolia. His words come in short bursts and phrases through my ears— reindeer, shaman, fishing, volcanoes, lakes, marmot meat, Swedish biologists, Karakorum, etc, etc. It's almost too much to take. I could have been with him. I could have chosen to scrap the expedition and just sit on my ass in the back of a van and get driven around to all the scenic points of Mongolia. He's seen more places in this country than I've seen, and he's been comfortable the whole time. He hasn't been thirsty for the past two weeks! He hasn't been in pain!

It takes a measured amount of self-control to keep my resentment from showing. "That sounds really cool. I almost wish I could have gone with you."

"What about you? How did it go?," Alain prods, waiting for some kind of adventurous tale from me.

"Wolves," I reply. "I had wolves around my tent one night." It's a true story.

During my stay in Beijing before I took the train to Mongolia, I spoke with several Chinese and Western people about my plans for a cross-country Mongolian expedition. Their reactions were all pretty similar. "That's quite an adventure." "You've got a lot of balls, man." And that sort of thing. But several of them also brought up the subject of wolves, as in "Aren't you afraid of all the wolves there?"

This took me by surprise, since I had never read anything about wolves in Mongolia. The Lonely Planet guide to Mongolia doesn't have a chapter on "wolf safety" or even mention them by name in the index. I had been to Mongolia before and I never heard about wolves. All the people I had met who took horses into the country-side for weeks at a time never mentioned wolves. Clearly, these people were misinformed, and I forgave them their ignorance, just as I would if I told an American that I was going to Canada and he said, "Watch out for the wolves." Please, can we keep it real, folks?

A month later and I was actually on the steppe, alone, with only my tent to protect me at night. And I heard wolves. I was only one day's golfing away from finishing hole two in Javkhlant, also known as Bayan-Ovoo. My spirits were higher than normal on this day because not only would I soon conclude the second of eighteen holes, but also because the Kherlen River had meandered its way back to the main road and I had an opportunity to camp near the river and fill up my water bottles without making a long trek. Adjacent to the river were bare but shrubby trees that provided some seclusion from passersby on the main road. Things were looking up. I had a few handfuls of peanuts for dinner, and then retired to my tent just as the sun began to dip below the horizon.

That's when I heard the wolves. And not just one lonely wolf howling longingly at the moon, like in the movies. This was a symphony of howls that began as a low drone and then increased in volume until it drowned out all other sounds. I had never heard anything like this before in my life. Maybe I had taken too few trips to Canada. I like dogs and I generally feel comfortable being around them. This misguided self-confidence and inexperience in the Great Outdoors may have accounted for my next move, which was to get out of the tent and try to get a look at these creatures. The lupine chorus continued to grow in intensity, and I continued to stand and wait until a prescient moment of clarity descended upon me and I decided that maybe it wasn't so smart for me to be trying to reenact a scene from *Dances with Wolves*. I've read about wolves and I know that they almost never attack humans, but there was something a little too unnatural about standing there waiting for them. I didn't want to end up as a candidate for a Darwin Award, the Internet-based accolade bestowed upon people who do something so stupid that they actually help prove the theory of natural selection when they perish. *Man tries to play fetch with wolves, then gets eaten.*

My thin nylon wall of protection made me feel more comfortable inside my tent, and still I got to enjoy that feeling that all campers crave: the feeling of being embedded in the very heart of nature, raw and untamed. Then I thought of Beijing, the warnings I received, and how stupid it was for me to presume that I know what I'm doing.

But I don't relay this part of the story to Alain.

"They were all around me!" I say, circling my arms above my head in a wild motion. It's an impressive story, and I'm glad I've got something positive to tell from my adventure instead of telling how I just couldn't hack the difficulties of the expedition any more.

"What would you have done if they attacked you?"

As Alain waits for his response, I notice a young woman in Western clothing glance up from her computer and gaze in my direction. She's obviously been eavesdropping. I don't mind because: (a) she's good-looking, and (b) I'm telling a really cool story that just has to sound impressive. But this does add a little pressure to my response.

"Um, well," I pause dramatically, although I'm not really sure what to say next. I had thought about this question not long after my encounter with the wolves, and didn't really come up with a satisfactory answer for myself. "I had my Swiss Army knife," I finally retort, laughing. I also get a laugh out of Alain and an amused smile from the girl at the computer. I make a mental note: the fact that I can laugh about an issue as serious as this shows how far from reality I'm drifting. It's great that I can make others laugh with the whole premise of my expedition, but I really should be taking the safety aspect of it more seriously. Instead, I plod along like Alice in Wonderland through my bizarre existence that I have created for myself. "Do you know where I can find a baby carriage?"

I relate to Alain the great vision that came to me a few nights ago while I was tossing and turning in my sleeping bag. A vision that lifted me from a moment of despair to one of epiphany. I would find a way to make this damn expedition work, one way or another. "Wheels," I explain. "That's what separated modern man from his predecessors—the invention of the wheel. Just like them, I've got too much to carry. So, I need wheels. And I was thinking of getting one of those really nice baby carriages and using the axles to make a cart. I could go up to the part of the city where we saw all those welders and get one of them to make me something. It would be pretty cheap."

I see the wheels in Alain's mind turning. "We should look at the State Department Store. I'm sure they've got something there." Like a true friend, he's playing along in my overly optimistic fantasy world. Although on the walk over to Mongolia's largest department store, he makes an observation that is completely realistic. "Man, if you thought you looked ridiculous already, hitting a golf ball across the country, then imagine what people will think when they see you pushing a baby carriage."

"They'll have even more pity on me," I reply. "Either that, or they'll be completely scared shitless by me."

The selection of baby strollers at the State Department Store is not as grand as I had hoped. They have a few of the four-wheeled variety, but no super-tricycle jogging strollers. And the wheels on the ones they have are about three inches in diameter, and they're plastic. I need big, sturdy, spoked wheels. This is a big letdown.

"How about at the Black Market?" Alain suggests.

The Black Market, known locally as *"khar zakh"* or as *"naran tuul,"* is not a virtual money-laundering enterprise, but an actual open-air market. Ulaan Baatar's largest, in fact, and it's been said that any single item that can be bought or sold anywhere in Mongolia can be found at the Black Market. They've got acres of fabrics, clothing, household goods, and electronics. You can buy an imitation Gucci handbag, the hind quarter of a goat, or a new cover for your cell phone. It's almost too big to see it all in one day, and the place is swarming with pickpockets. The market is both complete chaos and efficient commerce all at once. If there was any place to find some sturdy wheels for a makeshift golf cart, then this would be the place. Alain and I hopped in a taxi and made the four-kilometer journey to the southeast corner of town.

The market is teeming with activity, and we squeeze our way to the area where Alain thinks he's seen welders and other craftsmen who might be able to fabricate something for me. If only I can explain what I want and negotiate a reasonable price. On the way to the eastern edge of the market, I stop to look at some sunglasses. My current pair has gotten pretty banged up, and they now sit crooked on my face.

"How do these look?" I ask, turning toward Alain. He gives me the thumbs-up sign and turns away to cast his attention at someone walking by with a caged snake.

"Are these Adidas or Boss?" I ask the salesperson. One side of the glasses has the word Adidas printed on it, and the other side says Boss. These are two competing brands of sunglasses.

"Yes," comes the reply, my sarcasm completely lost.

"Okay, then, I'll take them." The poorly imitated, doubly brand-named glasses cost less than a dollar.

A minute later, I find myself looking at something much more valuable. This is no Chinese-made facsimile of modern Western fashion, but a product of Mongolian ingenuity. More important for me, it's a dream come true. Literally.

It's a tubular metal frame that forms a basket with a long handle, propped on top of two hard rubber wheels. It looks like a cross between a lawnmower and a dolly. It's painted blue, and the wheel hubs are bright orange. It's perfect. Alain looks at me inquisitively and I try to curb my exuberance as I tell him that I think this will do nicely. I don't want to lose any bargaining leverage by letting the seller know how eager I am to buy this thing.

I take it for a test spin by pushing it about twenty feet and then pulling it back. I kick the tires. This thing is a miracle. It is nearly the exact design that I had envisioned. And now I can just buy it without having to draw up diagrams and explain to a welder what I'm looking for. The answer to all my problems is right in front of me. The weight shall be lifted from my shoulders! The expedition shall continue! Golf Mongolia has wheels!

I settle on an amount that is the equivalent of fifteen dollars and proudly wheel away my new purchase from the market gates toward a waiting taxi. All the locals seem amused as I pass them, wondering what a foreigner can possibly do with a locally fabricated cart that countryside families would typically use for hauling milk cans or jugs of water from a nearby well to their gers.

If they only knew.

The English language has done an extraordinarily efficient job of categorizing and cataloging human emotions. Exhilaration, hope, anguish, dejection. These are all great words that sum up complex human feelings. But there is no word to describe how I feel now. No one term that could possibly represent the state of being where my emotional mind now lies.

Imagine a plague. Now, imagine that someone comes to lead you out of the plague. But then you realize that this person doesn't know any more about plagues than you do. And then you realize that you'll probably have to live with the plague after all, and you wonder why you were so gullible as to believe this person in the first place. It's a complex history of several emotions all rolled into a single feeling. It's a bad feeling; that much I can tell you. And I can also tell you that this is exactly how I feel now, sitting on the ground with my back propped up against my once-and-future savior, the golf cart.

It was supposed to be a revolutionary new addition to the Golf Mongolia ensemble. The answer to my plague of bodily pain. No longer would I lift the heavy load on and off my shoulders more than a hundred times a day. Instead, the burden would be rolled along with ease. My feet would sing. My shoulders would dance. I had found a way to carry on with the expedition when the point of collapse was desperately close. And I had let myself get swept away with enthusiasm, which is probably the reason why my emotional state now is nearing despondency.

This cart sucks. There's no way around it. It is just as much a pain in the ass to push across the grass as it was to carry the back-pack; I'm actually thinking of leaving it and carrying the pack on my shoulders again. It's true that the exhaustion comes from my forearms more than my shoulders, but the overall level of daily fatigue hasn't changed one bit. It's certainly not the answer to all my problems, like I had imagined it to be two days ago.

It was my optimism that provided the strength for my departure from Ulaan Baatar. I had spent five days in the relatively comfort-able confines of Mongolia's capital. I had dined on lasagne and kung pao chicken and washed them down with frosty mugs of cold beer. I had sipped café latte while devouring fresh-baked apple strudel. Compared to life in the countryside, this was heaven, and it took an awful lot of self-motivation to persuade myself to leave. My new cart played a big part in this. But now the facade of optimism has completely crumbled and reality has hit me again like a ton of bricks. This just isn't going to be easy.

If you've ever pushed a lawn mower up a steep slope of grass, then you know how I feel. Just imagine that the slope continues on for twenty-five kilometers and that the lawn mower is weighed down by sixty pounds of water, golf balls, and camping gear. This is my new challenge—learning how to handle the cart as I push it over clumps of grass and weeds and up and down gullies and slopes. It tends to list from side to side and bounce up and vibrate over every grass clump as I struggle to push it forward. Occasionally it hits a bump that it can't manage and stops dead, leaving my momentum to carry me into the metal handle that protrudes from the cart at a height exactly equal to that of my groin.

On a positive note, I've been able to keep my water supply in check, with three new plastic two-liter bottles that sit in a cardboard box in the back of the cart. The bottles are clear plastic and have a blue label with the name Aqua Minerale written in both Cyrillic and Roman script. As I read the label for a means of entertaining myself, I'm not shocked to learn that this company is a subsidiary of the Coca-Cola Corporation. I'm sure the company founders could have never imagined, though, that one of their products would be consumed near an isolated stretch of land in the middle of Khentii Province in central Mongolia.

I purchased the bottles on the morning I left Ulaan Baatar to return to the course. I had spent a couple days trying to figure out how I'd ever get back close to where I had left off golfing. Then I met Daka, an employee at one of the city's few coffee shops, who seemed willing to help me out, both as an excuse to practice her English and also because, I felt, she somehow seemed impressed by the fact that I wanted to hit a golf ball from one side of her country to the other. She was one of the few Mongolian people I had met so far who saw both the purpose and the irony in what I was doing. And she was extremely resourceful.

Daka introduced me to one of the waitresses who had a brother with a jeep who just happened to be heading to Öndörkhaan the next day. It was perfect. He said he could take me and all my gear, including my recently purchased water-carrier-cum-golf-cart, to the city for 30,000 tögrögs. This was about the price of three normal passenger fares if I were to take a shared van like the one I originally took to Choibalsan. This seemed pretty fair, since there was no way in hell I was going to cram myself into a van with twenty other people again, especially not with my new cart as additional cargo. And also because he would only be able to take one other passenger, where ordinarily he might have been able to get several people to pay him for the ride. We left early the next morning.

The downside in this was that he wouldn't be able to take me to the exact point where I had met George and the others, the place where I had stopped my golf progress. I reconciled this by realizing that on occasion, golf courses may change the layout of a particular hole because of environmental factors such as water damage or seasonal playability. And in such cases a provisional green is often used at a location that makes the overall distance of the hole a bit shorter.

That last thirty-seven miles of hole three was mostly through the flat and relatively lush floodplain of the river where the grass was dry and yellow, but also tall and thick. It would have been rough going, with many dozens of lost balls. And, to tell you the truth, there was no way in hell I was going to go backward. Hole three would just have to be shortened. And so, upon reaching Öndörkhaan, I immediately began playing toward Ulaan Baatar on hole four. That was when I was still optimistic about my new purchase.

A day later, the dejection phase of emotion had started to set in. My arms were tired from pushing the damn cart, and I began to realize that things weren't looking so good. This cart was not the savior I thought it would be, and maybe I should start thinking about another solution. The truth is, I had already thought about other solutions.

I had thought about buying a horse. But the problems with this option seemed to outweigh the benefits. I imagined having to tie up the horse every time I wanted to hit a shot or look for my ball. I imagined the horse running away with all my gear tied to its back. If you thought I looked ridiculous chasing my tent across the steppe, then imagine how funny it would be to see me chasing a horse. And finally, how could the horse survive if I could barely provide enough water for myself? I didn't want to end up with a dead horse on my hands. It's a bad round of golf when a horse dies on the course. No, a horse just wasn't the answer.

I had thought about camels. They don't need as much water as a horse. But I didn't know shit about camels, never mind how to train them or care for them. Can you imagine how frustrating it would be to have to pull on a stubborn camel just to get him to walk from shot to shot? It would be days of excruciating slow progress and enormous stress. A team of camels with a professional camel driver to care for them and keep them moving all day might work. But I had no idea where to find such a person, never mind the camels themselves. I had only seen one camel so far, leading me to believe that this was just too far north of the Gobi Desert to be camel country.

In an ideal world, I could set up a full expedition team the way that Roy Chapman Andrews did back in the 1920s. Andrews is the famous American explorer who led a series of five "Central Asiatic Expeditions" into the Gobi Desert of Mongolia between 1922 and 1930. The expeditions were sponsored by the American Museum of Natural History in New York and were designed to investigate the theory that mammals originated in Asia. Although he never recovered enough fossil evidence to support this theory, his expeditions did make some of the most ground-breaking (no pun intended) paleontological discoveries of their time. He unearthed nests of fossilized dinosaur eggs, found whole velociraptor skeletons, and discovered many new species of dinosaurs, including the *Protoceratops andrewsi.*

Andrews was also a celebrity in his time. He traveled the world and then traveled the circles of high society's elite, entertaining everyone with adventurous tales of woe from around the globe. It's been said that the character of Indiana Jones was based on the caricature of Roy Chapman Andrews. A lover of exploration myself, I'm naturally impressed with an explorer who ventured into Mongolia five times and became a celebrity. But I'm also struck by Andrews's organizational skills. Unlike me, he knew what he was doing, and he managed the expeditions in efficient and ingenious ways.

For example, the pure logistics of getting into the Gobi Desert and exploring a wide swath of territory for potential paleontological finds, all in a short window of good weather between the springtime dust storms and the impossibly harsh winter temperatures, was a challenge in itself. His solution was to drive a fleet of cars and trucks from Beijing into Mongolia and to supply them with gasoline and oil that was carried by a camel caravan that would rendezvous with the expedition team at several points. The challenges he overcame to succeed in these expeditions were legendary. But then again, he had a budget to work with that would translate into millions of dollars today.

This is where I can't help but be a little contemptuous of Andrews. I'm alone, and I have been alone since the genesis of this expedition. I've planned it all myself and mostly funded it all myself. Imagine what I could do with a million dollars. I could have a team of Land Cruisers accompanying me. Or even better, a fully loaded Winnebago! I'd have a cook, masseuse, golf coach, and team of videographers with me. I'd have a satellite phone that could link up to my Web site and provide continuous coverage of the expedition to the world. Things would be different.

But I don't have a million dollars, and this blue and orange golf cart is about the closest I'll come to mechanized transport. And at least I've got something to lean against when I sit on the ground and rest, like now.

I've been hitting the ball toward a distant row of mountains all day. I first saw the mountains this morning, just after I passed through the town of Mörön. It's a humbling feeling to be hitting a golf ball and then searching aimlessly for it amongst a herd of cows while standing within the borders of a town whose name resembles the word "moron." Just who is the moron, anyway?

But those mountains that appeared after I golfed over a small hill on the western edge of Mörön's town limits have been taunting me all day. I originally thought that they would provide a nice place to camp tonight, and I had my mind set on reaching them by sunset. But shot after shot and hour after hour, they just didn't get any closer to me. It's the same lesson I've learned several times now about the deceptive nature of judging distances here on the steppe. Nothing is as far as it seems—it's always farther.

With my backpack propped up in the front of the cart and the cardboard box in the back, I can get a tiny bit of shade if I squeeze myself up against the right wheel. It's only enough shade to cover a part of the upper half of one of my legs, but at least it's something. The sun has been consistently punishing each of the last three days, since I started on hole four. Aside from the mountains ahead, there are no features present on the horizon and shade is at a premium.

I'm lost in my indescribable emotional state, staring at a trail of ants that climb over my golf ball, when I hear a truck approaching. I'm sitting a mere fifty yards from the road and I'm easily visible. I'm not sure if it's a coincidence or not, but this ten-wheel flatbed truck with metal rails forming an enclosure over the bed has chosen this spot to come to rest. It may be repairs or it may just be a moment for the drivers to relax. I watch as four men empty out of the truck's cab and immediately begin executing some task as if they were following a carefully planned exercise. Two open the hood and work on the engine while the other two jump up into the open bed of the truck. In the back are several horses and a few camels. After a few minutes, their choreographed exercise comes to an end and they return to the shade of the truck's front seat and sit inside with the doors open. The driver lights a cigarette, exhales, and then yells in my direction.

I'm feeling a bit shy in my dejected and melancholy state, so I just wave to them. This will let them know that I can't understand what he's asking. Maybe they'll drive away and just let me mope a little longer.

But no, now they're yelling something else and a couple of them are waving their arms for me to come over there. I reluctantly rise from the ground and walk in their direction, realizing that even in my anti-social state, it'll be nice to sit somewhere out of the sun for a while.

We exchange greetings and get through the introductory questions such as where I'm going and where I've come from. Their high spirits and easy laughter are contagious, and, after a minute, my mood has gotten considerably better. I ask where they've come from.

"Sukhbaatar Province," one of them replies and smiles, showing a row of teeth with several conspicuous vacancies. "We're going to Ulaan Baatar. Do you want a ride?"

"No, I prefer to walk," I reply. "I'm very strong." This makes them all laugh. Then I join in the laughter. It's pretty hilarious pretending to be nonchalant about the difficulty of my task, and they pick up on this quickly. One of them reaches behind the seat and takes out a cardboard box that is full of pieces of dried meat. He places the open box in front of me as if to say, "Well, strongman, you better get some of this if you're going to have enough energy to make it."

He is so accurate with this thought, or maybe it's just my thought, that I reach in and pull out a greasy bone. The driver hands me a knife, and I cut off a few pieces of meat. It's not that bad, actually, and pretty soon all five of us have knives in our hands and we're all reaching into this cardboard box of dried mystery meat with our filthy hands and feasting away. It reminds me of standing around a barbecue grill with my buddies back in the United States after a few too many cans of beer, stuffing ourselves with ribs and chicken, forgoing any desire for vegetable or bread products. It must be an innate male-bonding phenomenon that transcends borders and cultures, men sharing cooked flesh.

"How much does it cost for a horse?" I ask, to break the silence.

"90,000 tögrögs." This is about eighty dollars. It's damn cheap for an entire animal, and the idea of obtaining a beast of burden crosses my mind again. "How about a camel?" I inquire.

"That's about 200,000 tögrögs," the guy with the missing teeth replies. It also seems like a good deal to me. On the other hand, I wonder how these guys are actually making a profit by transporting a few horses and camels all the way from the country's easternmost province to the capital and selling them for so little.

The guy next to me holds the cardboard box in front of me and shakes it, offering more meat. I dig in for a second helping. I haven't been eating much since I left the capital. It mostly boils down to the fact that I'm just so exhausted at night that I want to get out of the sun and lie down in my tent. This meat will actually make up a big portion of my caloric intake today. And how could I refuse to dig into a box of meat that's been sitting behind a truck

seat filled with four dirty, greasy Mongolian guys hauling camels?
It's almost too cool to be true.

"Julia Roberts."

"What?" I'm not quite sure if I heard the driver correctly.

"Julia Roberts . . . Ulaan Baatar." These are two of the words I
understand in his next sentence.

"Julia Roberts is in Ulaan Baatar?" I ask. "Right now?"

He nods his head. This is interesting. I know that the actress has
been in Mongolia before and filmed a documentary of her experience living in the Mongolian countryside. I've thought about trying
to get a celebrity involved in my expedition to help with the pub-
licity angle and to help move along the idea of raising money for a
charity. She would be a perfect candidate.

At this point, I lose myself in thought for a moment, wondering
how I could get in touch with her. I even go so far as to imagine her
walking or even golfing alongside me across the country. I've got a
two-person tent with me. There's plenty of space. I'd be a perfect
gentleman, of course. Shit, I can't remember if she's married or not.
Wasn't it Lyle Lovett? No, that was a long time ago. She might
actually be single now.

I snap out of my daydream and back into reality. "Keep it real,
André, keep it real," I tell myself. This guy probably doesn't know any
more than I do. How could he? I was just in Ulaan Baatar four days
ago and I didn't hear anything about Julia Roberts. This guy was in
Sukhbaatar aimag, for Christ's sake! He's definitely full of shit.

I lift a bone with my left hand, cut off a piece of meat with my right, and then toss the bone back into the box. I can't believe I got all worked up over Julia Roberts. I've got to stay focused and maintain my grip on reality.

I decide to start right away by saying farewell to my new friends and hitting another thirty shots today. That'll get me close to 140 shots for the day, the most I've done so far. I focus on the mountains ahead and then climb out of the truck. "Say hello to Julia for me," I say with a wave as the engine roars. The camels' humps bounce and sway as the truck sets off in a cloud of dust. A few kilometers short of the mountains, I stop after hitting 138 shots.

My east-to-west course through the first three holes paralleled the path of the Kherlen River. This is roughly the route of the main road linking Choibalsan and Öndörkhaan. But these two guiding features diverge in Öndörkhaan, the river continuing west before making a gradual right-hand turn and heading north, and the road making a direct diagonal cut across this arc before crossing paths with the river again near Baganuur. I had originally planned holes four and five to follow the river until it crossed the road again, and then hole six would follow the main trail to Ulaan Baatar. I had learned a couple things, however, in the first several days of the expedition that made me rethink this plan.

First, the terrain directly adjacent to the river was often filled with tall, wispy grass, reeds, and low shrubs. Second, the road almost always followed terrain that was high and dry, with limited vegetation. This second type of terrain is much more conducive to golf. And with the ability to carry up to seven liters of water in my new cart, the advantages of staying close to the river were diminished. I chose to follow the road.

It's now July 5, nine days since I left Öndörkhaan. The choice to follow the road was a smart one and the golfing conditions have generally been excellent. My progress has also been excellent. Yesterday I golfed twenty-four kilometers and hit 140 shots without pushing myself to the limit. After nearly a month of walking and whacking, I finally feel like I'm getting in shape. A layer of fat has certainly been eliminated from my previously conspicuous beer belly, and the blisters on my hands and feet have finally turned into calluses.

The increase in my energy level may also have something to do with the fact that I've been eating better lately. This stretch of road has had frequent opportunities for dining out. I've visited three roadside *guanzes* in the past three days. The guanzes are gers located near the road where people can stop for a hot meal while driving across the country. Sometimes there are clusters of guanzes forming a small town, and sometimes they're randomly placed along the road. But they're always stocked with hot Mongolian milk tea, and they can usually make a handful of traditional Mongolian meals to order. *Tsuivan* is a popular choice in these establishments. It's made from fried homemade noodles and chunks of mutton, with a few onion pieces tossed into the mix. Other common offerings from these guanzes are *gulyash* (mutton stew served with rice), *guriltai shöl* (mutton-and-noodle soup), and *banshtai shöl* (mutton-dumpling soup). I've opted for banshtai shöl in every guanz I've stopped in. It's one of the Mongolian dishes that I can always identify and that is always consistent. And I can say "banshtai shöl" with a perfect Mongolian accent now. What I like most about the soup is that not only does it have mutton-filled dumplings, but it also has pieces of mutton mixed into the broth. It's as if any respectable meat-eating Mongolian just wouldn't be satisfied with the amount of meat in the dumplings alone, so they had to add more meat to the broth.

I also visited a small food shop selling various groceries yesterday in the small town I passed through. They had copious amounts of candy, all individually wrapped like the penny candy that I used to buy from my local five-and-dime store as a kid. They had a few jars of pickled products from Russia, lots of little bags of fried dough and other bread-like foods, and at least ten different brands of Mongolian vodka. But what caught my eye instantly was the open-top box of Snickers candy bars. Snickers bars are a long-standing favorite of mine in the candy bar world, and the sight of those

brown and blue wrappers brought a smile to my face. They had six
of them left, and I bought all six. It may have been my body's way of
telling me it needed more calories, or it may have been an irresistible
urge to have and hold something familiar. The Snickers bars provided a link for me back to my own culture and land. In an alien
world of chaos and confusion, where many travelers find themselves
when abroad, a simple familiar food or drink can serve as a powerful
emotional tool in restoring order and comfort. I don't doubt that this
was the exact phenomenon that was taking place in me when I
decided to buy the tiny store out of all their Snickers bars. And hey,
the peanuts, chocolate, and nougat are damn good together.

I'm contemplating having one at this very moment, but instead
reach deep into my backpack for a can of tuna fish. The tuna was
another key purchase that I made while I was back in Ulaan Baatar.
It's chunk light tuna in oil, and upon opening the can, I carefully lift
it to my mouth and drink all the oil that the tuna is packed in. This
means I'll get at least 500 calories out of this one can. It's the kind of
thing that I never, in my entire life, would have dreamed of doing.
Back in the days when I was watching what I ate, I always used to
buy tuna in water. The pure idea of drinking off all the oil in the
can was preposterous. But I'll be damned if that isn't some great-
tasting shit.

The oily tuna makes up my lunch today. I've just taken a break
after golfing thirty-two consecutive shots without losing a golf ball.
It's a wide valley with short hills flanking both sides where I sit

now. The valley forms a perfectly straight path that I've been following for several kilometers, and, looking ahead, it will go on for a few more. The remarkable thing about this valley is its perfect short grass. This is the best terrain that I've seen yet, and I've made excellent progress because I can spot my ball every time as soon as I walk within twenty yards of it. This is exactly the kind of terrain that I'm hoping to see more of in the weeks to come.

I'm wearing shorts, so I wipe the tuna grease onto my bare legs as a sort of skin moisturizer and then pick up my club and resume my golf ritual. The three-iron rests in the back of my cart with the grip against the cart's handle for easy access. I lift the club and then spot the ball onto a playable tuft of grass. After one practice swing, I line up my next shot, aimed straight down the center of the valley. Ahead of me and slightly to the left, I can see the dust of a traveling vehicle making its way along one of the many parallel roads in this valley. It's the fourth vehicle I've seen today; a noticeable increase in traffic. Swack! I take a full swing and look up to track the flight of the ball. My golf game has been in a consistently good groove lately. The three-iron feels like a natural extension of my arms by now, and it's rare for me to hit a bad shot.

After just ten more swings, I notice something interesting—the clear delineation of a river against the backdrop of some low mountains. It's hard to tell from this distance just how big it might be, but I'm excited because this could be the Kherlen. After another hour of progress, I spot a bridge.

Infrastructure is sparse in Mongolia, and I know that there is probably only one bridge on this stretch of the Kherlen River. This has to be the bridge along the main road that links Khentii Province to Töv Province. I know this bridge well, because I've been over it three times already. A month ago, as Alain and I were on our way to Choibalsan, I stood only a hundred meters from this bridge and studied its architectural features while we waited for the van to resume its journey after a pit stop.

The sight of this bridge stirs up an emotional reaction inside me. It's the same feeling I used to get as a child when, traveling back home from far away, I would spot a familiar landmark. Practically, it meant that I wasn't far from home; but it also made me feel comforted, and safe. This bridge is my link to familiar territory—the road back to Ulaan Baatar. The sight of the bridge also brings surprise, because I never thought I would have been here after only nine days of golfing from Öndörkhaan. My determined progress has paid off.

My next fifteen shots cross an area of sandy dunes that appear to have been caused by the destruction of the vegetation by vehicular traffic. It's a reminder of how fragile the landscape is and how quickly grasslands can turn into desert if they are disturbed or over-grazed. And, more noticeably, it makes the golfing a little more difficult. Soon, I find myself at the foot of the bridge, wondering how exactly I'm going to cross it, or more accurately, how I'm going to *golf* it. After some deliberation, I decide against rolling the ball across the bridge like a giant mini-golf hole and instead I attempt to hit the ball across the river. It's difficult to judge exactly how far it is, but I know I'll need a full three-iron to make it safely across. I take a stronger than normal swing.

If I were skipping stones, I might receive some hardy applause, because my golf ball bounces across the surface of the water several times before disappearing below the surface like a Jacques Cousteau reverse roll off the edge of a boat. I stand silently, poised with the golf club in my hand, staring at the water with utter disbelief. I'm golfing across Mongolia, one of the driest countries in East Asia, and I lose a ball in a water hazard. My next move is to do what any real golfer would do, any golfer who doesn't play for money or profess to actually be good at the game. I take a mulligan.

I understand that nongolfers might look at the word *mulligan* with some curiosity. To clear things up immediately, I'll give the Webster's definition: "Mulligan—*Golf.* A shot not counted against the score, permitted in unofficial play to a player whose previous shot was poor." In other words, it's a do-over, a chance at redemption, an opportunity to erase the past and start again with a clean slate. Unlike many people in the world, golfers have the chance to rewrite history. But don't get me wrong, we don't abuse this superpower ordained on us by the gods of golf. In typical non-competitive play, a golfer will only be allowed one mulligan per round. This is a check against abuse, sort of like a genie only granting three wishes instead of an unlimited amount. It keeps us humble.

It's unclear where the term *mulligan* comes from, but there are many theories and urban legends revolving around the etymology of this word. Most have to do with someone named Mulligan who was notorious for asking his partners for second chances after he hit a poor shot. In some versions, Mr. Mulligan was a doctor, and in others he was a locker room attendant. One theory says the word comes from the fact that Mulligan is a common Irish name and that during a time when ethnic slurs were more common, the WASP country-club types would refer to this form of cheating as taking a Mulligan. But the version I like the most traces the roots of the word back to the saloons of the early twentieth century, whose bartenders would occasionally place a free bottle of booze on the counter for anyone's taking. This bottle was called a Mulligan. Golfers, who presumably spent a fair share of their time in saloons before and after playing golf, adapted this term that meant "something free" to the golf course and the practice of occasionally giving a "free shot" that wasn't counted against the score.

I've golfed nearly five hundred kilometers so far and hit nearly three thousand shots. If anyone deserves a mulligan, I rationalize, it's me. I tee up another ball on a few blades of grass poking out of the sand, and I let it rip. The ball flies lazily across the river and lands amid some rocks on the other shore. I have officially completed the golf in Khentii Province, the second province of seven that I will cross on my way to the far west. It's a significant milestone for me.

After I roll my cart across the bridge and find my ball, it's only a dozen more shots until I'm standing next to a small concrete building, its exterior once painted white, but now showing years of weathering and exposure to the clouds of dust from passing vehicles. It's a decrepit-looking structure, but I'm pleased to be here because I know that this has to be a guanz and an opportunity for another hot meal. I step inside and proceed to a small window that opens to a kitchen. A young woman looks in my direction, so I make a motion with my hand that shows me lifting food to my mouth and I say the word *khool* which means, simply, "food." From what I understand of her response, they only have one thing, *khar shöl*. The last part of it means soup, and I think the first word means "black." Black soup can't be that bad, so I order a bowl and take a seat at one of three long tables with colorful plastic tablecloths. The one on my table has a Hello Kitty motif.

Sitting at another of the tables are two well-dressed men with empty bowls in front of them. They look in my direction, and one of them addresses me in English.

"Hello," he says. "How are you doing?"

This is the first time I've heard English in ten days, and I respond eagerly. "I'm fine. It's not too hot today. They only have black soup on the menu, but they've got bottles of water and juice for sale," I ramble. There's so much that I want to say that I just don't know where to begin. I'm sure I must sound like a raving idiot to these guys, but they were the ones who started the conversation, so I can't help it. "I've been walking for nine days straight, well, golfing actually. I'm hitting a ball across the country. I started in Choibalsan but I'm coming from Öndörkhaan now. It's taken nine days to get here from Öndörkhaan."

"Oh, that sounds interesting," he replies with an enthusiasm that shows some effort. "We're from Japan and we're here on business. We're going to Khentii province now." The second man lifts his head to speak. "Did you say that you were . . . golfing?"

The fact that they're from Japan only generates more enthusiasm in my speech, because—I would probably never say this if I weren't in the middle of Mongolia—I feel like I share a common culture with them. They can understand what I'm doing. They know the game of golf and the spirit of adventure. They can probably appreciate all the aspects of my adventure: the difficulty, the originality, and the absurdity.

"Yes, I'm actually hitting a golf ball all the way across Mongolia," I say proudly. I then proceed to explain the logistics and some of my experiences, and eventually I lead them outside to see my cart. "I keep all the water here, and I lean my pack against the front so that it's a little front-heavy. That way I can push down on the handle as I walk and the cart stays balanced." I perform a small demonstration of how I balance the cart on its two wheels as I walk. They're a captive audience, but I think they're genuinely impressed now. Christ, who wouldn't be impressed? I'm sure they never thought they'd meet an American out here in eastern Mongolia who was golfing across the country.

We're soon joined by their Mongolian driver/translator, who appears to be curious about what's going on. I sense that he's a little apprehensive about joining in the conversation. His job is to explain things about his country, and I sense that he's a little baffled by the filthy, bedraggled foreigner with a backpack and golf club sticking out of a Mongolian water-cart. He says a few words in Japanese, and then the other two men turn to me and reach out their hands.

"Good luck. Maybe we'll see you on TV in Japan."

"I hope so," I reply as I shake their hands. "Good luck to you, too!"

I return inside to find a bowl of meat-filled broth on the table where I was sitting. The young woman pokes her head out of the service window and, with a nod of her head and a small hand gesture, she assures me that the soup is indeed mine. I'm sure that she's curious about me also, my having arrived on foot with no driver, guide, or translator. But smiles and hand gestures are all we have as common communication tools, and a real conversation is impossible. Since the brief encounter with the Japanese has ended, I'm left with only myself to talk to.

Later that day, camped in a low spot that is out of sight of the main road, I catch myself doing something I've never done before: I'm talking out loud to myself. Actually saying words, audibly, as I would if someone else were present. This is shocking to me, because I always thought that the practice was reserved for people with some kind of mental abnormality. We all think to ourselves; but to actually speak the words out loud, that's just weird. My conversation with the Japanese guys today made me realize just how little social contact I've had recently. Perhaps the phenomenon of talking to myself is some kind of subconscious psychological defense mechanism that only kicks in during times of solitude.

We've seen prisoners in solitary confinement and castaways on deserted islands talk to themselves in the movies, and we don't think twice about it. It's almost expected of them. But these people are also typically portrayed as a tad loony. Obviously no one can hear them, so why would they be speaking out loud if they were sane? This is the part that worries me. How does one know if he's going crazy, if there's no one else around to hear him? There's no objective opinion. His own mind is the suspect, but it's also the judge and jury. And quite frankly, who in their right mind would pronounce their right mind wrong? And how could they tell the difference if they weren't in their right mind? This is a depressing subject for me to be dwelling on alone, so I tell myself (silently) that I should stop talking to myself. I don't want to take any chances.

The mental-health issue has come up before in my self-analytical thoughts. Last night I heard some bizarre high-pitched noises that I couldn't identify, and for some reason I thought of aliens. I wondered what would happen if I were abducted by aliens, probed and tested, and then returned to my tent. Who could I possibly tell this story to? MAN GOLFING ACROSS MONGOLIA GETS ABDUCTED BY ALIENS is hardly the type of headline that anyone would take seriously. I'd be forced to keep this incredible experience to myself for fear that people would think I was crazy. Ironically, keeping it to myself probably would drive me crazy. It's a classic no-win situation, and after some time I began hoping that the strange noises would just stop and that no aliens would visit my tent.

The solitude of my expedition has been an unexpected challenge. I'd prepared myself for the physical difficulty (not prepared very well, I must admit) and for the practical challenges that I would face, but I hadn't expected any mental challenges. The effects of solitude have caught me off guard and left me with another burden that I must somehow find a way to carry. But I try not to think of those challenges now, and instead I focus on the good news. I made real progress today. Today, I crossed a bridge.

L ittle Lake sounds like the kind of name you'd give to a quaint New England town nestled on the shores of a freshwater pond that was fed by mountain streams. Perhaps there would be a general store, a small but quaint post office where you knew the postmaster's name, and maybe a covered bridge. But "Little Lake" is translated as "Baganuur" in Mongolian, and Baganuur is a city of 20,000 people in eastern Töv Province that is unquestionably a city of industry. There is nothing quaint whatsoever about Baganuur.

The city's raison d'être is the enormous opencut coal mine nearby. Like many of Mongolia's cities, it only became a city when large-scale industrialization and mining activities ramped up in the last century with an influx of foreign aid from the Soviet Union. As the mines grew, workers needed to be housed, and cities were born.

Baganuur was also home to a Soviet military base that now lies abandoned. The area surrounding the city is littered with dilapidated structures that have been deserted and looted for structural materials. The city gives the impression that it was once an important and proud center of industrial and military activity in the region and has since slipped into depression. This may not actually be true, because I do see trucks roaring to and fro and large smokestacks billowing out plumes of exhaust. Perhaps I want to believe that a city with the name "Little Lake" must have been more charming at one point in its history. And I still haven't seen any trace of a lake yet.

Just like at Choibalsan a month earlier, among the rubble and trash of the industrial-zone suburbs, it's been difficult for me to find my lone golf ball after each shot. I've lost several balls since I started this morning, and I've become increasingly frustrated with the abundance of small white objects that dot the landscape. Also frustrating is the fact that I can't tell which direction to go. There are dozens of roads continuously crisscrossing my path, without a clear indication of which one is the actual main thoroughfare that leads to Ulaan Baatar. It's a confusing place.

Eventually, I end up near a chain of several enormous mountains. Except that they're not mountains at all: they're piles of excavation tailings from the mines. Dump trucks and bulldozers roll up and down these mountains in a steady pace, helping the mountains grow ever larger. The ominous feeling and the size and scale of this operation are daunting. I've taken a wrong turn somewhere, and this is no place for a lost golfer to be trying to play through. I can't see any way out of this mess but to march toward the outline of the city center in hopes of finding the main road again. I want to be sure that I'm headed in the right direction and that I get a chance to stop at a small store to restock my supplies. Finding the main road is paramount in achieving these objectives.

I mark my coordinates on my GPS receiver and write down the distance I've traveled and number of shots I've hit so far today. The mountains of excavated earth and related heavy-equipment traffic are an industrial hazard, and I plan to place my ball on the other side of its limits. I didn't come to Mongolia to play golf through an industrial wasteland. I could have done that in New Jersey.

I walk across dirt lots filled with piles of brown and gray earth that have been unloaded out of the back of dump trucks like piles of mining excrement. I cross drainage ditches and pass through openings in crumbling concrete walls. I push my cart along the side of dirt roads and in between piles of trash that have been dumped in the fields outside the city limits. I push the cart steadily for an hour and a half to leave this ugly landscape behind and return to the open pastures where the game of golf can naturally blend with the earth. The animal dung, the difficulty of pushing my cart, and the unquenchable thirst are known obstacles that I have learned to overcome, but I need a clean, unspoiled terrain to golf in. That's all I ask.

With the industrial environment safely behind me, I resume play amidst a field of sheep, who have momentarily stopped their grazing to stare at the strange cart being pushed across the land by a man wearing a light green sun-bleached hat and Adidas Boss sunglasses. Baganuur fades away behind me as I progress westward. A steady stream of cars and trucks zooms by on the asphalt road that leads to the capital (a steady stream means about one car every five minutes). I use this road as a guide, and I golf on a parallel path about two hundred yards from it. It's comforting to see the cars and trucks roll past and head off toward the horizon. It means that there is no doubt that I'm going in the correct direction. Back in Dornod Province, where there was scant traffic and mazes of meandering dirt tracks, I never had this luxury of certainty that I wasn't getting lost. It was a constant thorn of stress that nagged me. But here I can concentrate on my golf progress without these ancillary worries.

I stop to rest and dig out another can of oil-soaked tuna from my backpack. I sit on one wheel of my cart and stretch my legs out in front of me, digging my heels into the ground so that the cart doesn't start rolling to one side or the other. With the tuna as a focus of solitary enjoyment, I rest my mind and enjoy the peace and quiet of Mongolia. I continue daydreaming until my attention is turned to a distant rumbling. It's a sound so low in wavelength that I can almost feel my body vibrate. The sound grows until I can actually feel the earth start to shake. Looking back toward Baganuur, I notice a low cloud of dust. I stay focused on the cloud and watch it grow taller and closer as the seconds tick by. I stand up for a better look.

I peer curiously in the direction of the dust cloud until I see a horse and rider appear on the ridge of a hill. He's riding directly toward me. Then a second rider appears, and then several more. Soon, dozens of horse riders are cresting the hill and charging directly toward me as the cacophony of hoofbeats grows. I feel like I'm in the middle of a battle scene in a Kurosawa film, with thousands of warriors on horseback appearing from behind a hill in a slow trickle and then overwhelming the screen.

I hold my three-iron protectively until the first rider passes me. He's a boy of about eight years of age. As the other riders approach and then race by me on both sides, I notice that they're all young boys and girls wearing colorful outfits and numbers. The boys hoot and holler as they ride past and stare at me curiously. Somehow I had placed myself in the middle of a long-distance horse race and these kids are just as surprised to see me there as I am to see them.

Several vehicles with banners flying from their rooftops pass by me, and then I notice that some of them have video cameras pointed at the racers. The amount of dust in the air thickens until I begin to worry that the jockeys won't see me. But a minute later, the line of horses has dwindled and the dust finally begins to settle.

This was a Naadam horse race. Naadam is an annual competition of the "three manly sports" of archery, wrestling, and horseracing. Most Mongolians eagerly anticipate the national Naadam competition and festival in Ulaan Baatar, which begins on July 11. But many smaller cities or counties hold their own Naadam festivals one or two weeks before or after the national festival. Apparently, the Baganuur festival is taking place today. I'm tempted to trek back to the city and stay for a day to watch some of the festivities, but I know that I'll be in Ulaan Baatar for the big event if I can continue golfing at my current pace. That's the place to be next week, and I need to keep moving if I'm to make it.

I finish the day a few hours later after hitting 149 shots. I would have gone for 150, but I lost my tenth golf ball of the day just as I reached a low swale, out of sight from the road—a perfect spot to pitch my tent. The end of golfing for the day also means that hole five is now complete. This milestone itself is a confidence-building achievement. I am now five-eighteenths of the way across the country. That's nearly 28 percent of the golf course completed. But more significantly, Ulaan Baatar is within my reach. There are people I know in Ulaan Baatar. Familiar bars and restaurants, a comfortable bed in a guesthouse, and a chance to gather my thoughts on this expedition all await me if I can just make it another hundred kilometers.

Not long after I set up my tent, an ominous row of black clouds begins to creep across the sky, and I feel the first few drops of rain.

It takes about five seconds for these few drops to turn into thousands of drops as the storm starts suddenly and forcefully. I dive into my tent and zip all the flaps as tight to the ground as they'll go and wait out the storm. My tent shakes in the wind, and the wall of water that splatters the nylon rain fly makes a sound like a thousand ball bearings being poured onto an aluminum pan. A few drops make their way through a seam on the top of my tent and drip down through the mesh netting of the tent's inner wall and onto my sleeping bag. There's nothing I can do but wait for nature to run her course and the storm to pass. And of course I can worry about lightning in the meantime.

My tent and the little metal cart sitting outside are literally the only anomalies on this treeless plain of short grass and scrubby weeds. If lightning were looking for targets like a seagull flying over an outdoor table at a seafood restaurant, I'd be an obvious choice. In practical terms, the only choice. This is one consideration that I hadn't thought about too much when planning my expedition. I never thought of lightning as being one of the practical dangers that I should prepare myself for. But I should have.

According to NASA, there are more than two thousand thunderstorms active in the world at any given moment. These storms produce about a hundred lightning flashes per second. That's more than three billion lightning strikes per year! On average, more than a hundred people die every year from lightning strikes in the United States alone. Hundreds more are stuck by lightning and survive. But most unnerving is the fact that golfers are particularly prone to being struck by lightning.

The National Oceanic and Atmospheric Administration (NOAA) has concluded that five percent of lightning fatalities are golf-related. In 1975, Lee Trevino and two other golfers were struck by lightning at the Western Open in Illinois. In 1991, a spectator at the U.S. Open at Hazeltine was struck and killed by lightning. Later that year, another spectator was killed by lightning at the PGA Championship. Yet many golfers still don't take lightning seriously. There's the old joke that says when there's lightning, you should take a one-iron out of your bag, because even God can't hit a one-iron.

But here I am now in a country that resembles one enormous golf course, in the middle of my third thunderstorm in the past four days. I should be worried. I have nowhere to go. NOAA recommends that if you're nowhere near a safe location in a lightning storm, then you should go into the Lightning Desperation Position. This is essentially squatting down, bending your head and neck, and kissing your ass good-bye. I would feel completely ridiculous doing that now in my tent, so instead I watch the little drips of water splash onto my sleeping bag and cause the perimeter of the water stain to grow. Mercifully, the storm passes, and thirty minutes later I can see the sun's rays poking out just above the horizon. My time has not yet come.

For the next three days, I golf like a madman. I push myself for ten hours a day up and over the rolling hills of Mongolia's central province on a mission to reach the city. This stretch of road is also part of the Millennium Road, and much of it has already been upgraded or is now under construction. One feature of the newly completed stretches of highway are the markers that are placed every kilometer, letting drivers know the exact distance to Ulaan Baatar. I've tried not to pay much attention to these signs, but I've had to cross the road a few times in search of better golfing conditions and I can't help but sneak a peek whenever I get the chance. The numbers are small enough to feel good about, considering the distances that I've already covered.

The closer I get to the capital, the fewer encounters I seem to be having with locals. Almost no one has approached me, and I haven't visited any families since Khentii Province. I reason that it's not as odd for a foreigner to be here in this part of the country, and also that the general increase in population density makes people less friendly and less trusting. I've had more contact with construction workers and engineers than anyone else recently, and this is probably because of my interest in their work.

Years ago, I worked for a contractor that built highways and bridges. This was where I gained most of my experience in the construction industry, long before I became an engineer. I started out as a laborer and then eventually became a foreman, working on a variety of projects, from site developments to sewer pipelines to interstate highways. And on all of these projects, I worked closely with heavy earth-moving equipment. The sound of an excavator's diesel engine roaring as it tosses bucketloads of earth and rock into a waiting dump truck, or the sound of a dozer's tracks clacking as it levels a pile of rubble into a uniformly smooth surface, will always represent sounds of nostalgia for me. And I can almost never resist having a look when there is a construction project nearby. At exactly eighty-eight kilometers from Ulaan Baatar, I had my chance.

A large area of tall reeds and dry caked earth forced me to begin angling my shots toward the road in the hope that I would find better grass there or on the other side. As I approached the partially constructed roadway, which sat about six feet higher than the surrounding terrain, I saw two men walking along the top of the roadway. I decided to climb up and have a look at the construction progress and talk to these guys.

"Sain Bainuu?" I was getting good at this by now.

"Sain, sain bainuu?" they both reply. I'm about to launch into my familiar mime routine with a bit of broken Mongolian thrown in for good measure when one of them catches me off guard.

"Where are you from?" he says in English.

"I'm from the United States," I reply enthusiastically. A real conversation in English is much more than I had hoped for. "I'm an engineer. I wanted to see how the road construction was going." I look down and notice that one of them is holding a device that is easily recognizable to me. It's a nuclear-density gauge. These machines are about the size and weight of a sewing machine and

I GOLFED ACROSS MONGOLIA

are commonly used to test the density of compacted soil on construction projects.

"I am an engineer also," the older of the two men replies; "I am from Japan." This doesn't surprise me, since the Japanese government is funding a big chunk of the construction cost of this new road.

"How are the tests coming out?"

"They're fine," he says and shows me a clipboard with columns of data. I scan the numbers and I'm able to decipher most of it, even though it's in metric, because the test results of all density tests are expressed as a percentage of optimum. I see several values that look a bit low to me and I point them out.

"What about these?" I ask with a laugh.

The Japanese engineer also laughs as if to say, "Oh, don't worry about those. It's hard enough to get any passing tests, never mind getting every test to pass."

I can understand his situation. It must be extremely difficult to enforce high quality control on a project with a limited budget and a workforce with limited experience. I've looked at some of the construction sites around Ulaan Baatar. The quality of the work leaves a lot to be desired, never mind the safety practices. But one way or another, this road will carry vehicles across Mongolia, potholes notwithstanding.

I descend back down the dirt slope to my parked cart with a feeling of reverence for the days when my existence was so simple.

All I had to do a few years ago was get up and go to work every morning. I didn't have to worry about dying of thirst or getting attacked by wolves or even finding decent terrain to golf across. I didn't have to push this stupid cart or sit through thunderstorms in my tent. But then again, I didn't get to golf all day.

I return to my golf ball, lying docilely next to my cart. I tee it up on a clump of low weeds and then I let it rip. "That felt good," I tell myself. "Never in my life, on any construction project, did it *ever* feel that good to take a density test." I haven't got it that bad.

According to the Mongolian government, almost 230,000 tourists visited Mongolia in the year 2002. It should be noted that about two-thirds of these were from China and Russia, Mongolia's neighboring countries and main trading partners. That leaves about 70,000 tourists from the rest of the world—in the entire year. By contrast, France receives 211,000 tourists every *day*. It's safe to say that Mongolia is not a top tourist destination. But the vast majority of intrepid international travelers who actually make it to visit this country, come for the Naadam Festival.

The city's hotels get booked solid, the beer and pizza joints fill up, and the streets are alive with souvenir sellers. There is a general

air of festivity around Ulaan Baatar during Naadam, and this was
the air I walked into when I arrived on the outskirts of the city a
day ago. After two weeks of near solitude on the featureless steppe,
it was almost too much for my senses to take.

I checked into a guest house and luckily secured the last bed that
was available. Later in the evening, two other travelers who arrived
after me had to sleep on the floor. And this was a guesthouse with
dozens of beds, most of which had been empty in my previous stays
here. It was chaos, but I was high on life. I had hundreds of reasons
to be happy, and foremost among them were the hot shower and
cold beer that I enjoyed not long after my arrival. I had completed
another stretch of the course and reached the one-third point in my
journey. Here, in the capital city, I could send e-mail to family and
friends. And I could tell my story to dozens of my fellow guests, all
willing listeners intrigued by the tale of a man who was in the
middle of golfing across the country. Some even stuck around to
hear the story twice. Among them was John, a tall lanky Canadian
in his early twenties.

"That's the most fucked-up thing I've ever heard. I've got to buy
you a beer." After two weeks of nothing but tepid water to drink,
an invitation to a cold beer was one I couldn't refuse. We dug up
our shoes from the pile of footwear near the guesthouse door and
headed to an establishment that John recommended called Greenland, an Oktoberfest-style outdoor tent with long wooden tables.

John was keenly interested in how and what I ate and how I

managed to navigate in the countryside. "You drank the oil from the tuna can? Oh, that's a good one. What about mutton? Did you carry any along?"

"I don't think it would have lasted in my backpack. And I managed to get a lot of hot meals from families that I met or from guanzes. There was plenty of mutton in there. I didn't need to carry more."

John finishes his pint of Chinggis lager and lights his third cigarette. He appears confident and naive at the same time, his mannerisms slightly dorky but casually cool. I have a hard time categorizing him, except to say that he's hyperactive, and very generous. "Let me get you another beer," he offers before turning quickly away to catch the attention of a waitress. "I've got to ask your opinion on something."

John takes a rare moment of silence and stillness before stating his thesis. "I want to take a horse across the country. I've got about three weeks left on my visa. How far do you think I could make it?" He draws deeply on his cigarette and stubs it into an ashtray. He gazes at me expectantly.

"I don't know. Maybe . . . a few hun— do you know how to ride a horse?" I feel the urge to ask the obvious.

"I've ridden a couple times. It's not really that hard. I'm more worried about what I'm going to bring for food."

I suddenly feel like my advice is seriously needed. "You should get some good maps. There's a great store about a mile from here.

It's called the Map Shop, or something like that. I'll draw you a map and show you how to get there. The maps they have are written in Mongolian, so you can show them to any of the locals and they'll be able to help you. You should try to follow a river. Do you have a camp stove?"

All of John's answers lead me to one conclusion: he's completely unprepared. He doesn't *really* know how to ride a horse, he doesn't know where he's going or what he's going to eat, and he doesn't own any camping equipment. He's going to get lost, his horse is going to run away with all his stuff at night, and he's going to have an extremely sore ass if he survives that long. But he seems determined to do this and there's no way for me to stop him, or his enthusiasm.

"I met this Israeli guy who's going to give me a bunch of equipment. He rode a horse for a couple weeks. He's got the saddle and all the gear for the horse that he's going to sell to me." John continues excitedly telling me about his plans, half-assed as they are, before he turns the conversation back to me. "So, you carried all your stuff in your backpack?"

"I did for the first two and a half weeks," I explain, "then I bought a cart in Ulaan Baatar and I pushed all my shit in that for the next two weeks."

"How did that work out?"

"Like crap. I gave the cart away as soon as I reached Ulaan Baatar. I couldn't stand the sight of the thing any more. It completely sucked."

It's all true. There's a giant gateway arch at the city limits with the words "ulaan baatar" spanning its entire width across the two-lane road where toll collectors hit up select motorists for a 50-cent tithe. Reaching that point was one of the happiest moments of my life. The toll workers stared curiously as I pushed my belongings under the arch and directly to a small roadside store. What I did next, I hadn't planned or even thought about, but there was no hesitation in my actions. I approached the first person I saw, a middle-aged woman, removed my backpack and golf club from the cart, and gently offered it to her. Then I turned and flagged a taxi that was miraculously passing through this remote part of the suburbs and headed into the city center, beaming a wide smile the whole time.

"So, what are you going to do now?" asks John.

I haven't got this part figured out yet, and I've avoided thinking about it. "I need a caddy. Maybe I'll buy a yak and call it my Caddy-yak." It's a joke that my friend Ian came up with a few months ago while I was planning this whole thing. It's corny, but it always gets a few laughs, so I feel justified in plagiarizing it.

"You need a camel, dude. Yeah, definitely a camel." John lets out a couple of high-pitched laughs as if the image of me taking a camel across Mongolia is completely ridiculous. What's ridiculous is the idea of him heading off on a horse into the Mongolian countryside without a clue what he's doing. But I don't return his laughter.

"Yeah, well, I thought about a camel, but I—"

John interrupts me as he holds another cigarette in his left hand, poised in front of his mouth, with a ready lighter in his right hand. "Have you been to the UB Palace? That place is going to be completely packed tonight. We oughta go."

He's referring to Ulaan Baatar's largest disco. I had actually been there once, two years earlier. It's an enormous place with a laser light system, a booming sound system, and a dance floor and three levels of tables filled with Ulaan Baatar's youth, paying inflated prices for Korean beer. I remember being impressed by the place, especially in light of the seemingly lifeless daytime personality of the capital city. They were playing all European and American pop songs, a reminder that it never takes long for the youth of a nation to embrace popular international culture, despite other changes in society and government moving much more slowly.

"Yeah, maybe I'll be up for it. I'll have to see how I feel after this beer." The truth is that after two sips from my second pint, I'm already catching a buzz. Aside from the few days in Ulaan Baatar two weeks ago, I haven't had any alcohol in a month and my tolerance has taken a significant dip.

"I'd like to go to the Naadam tomorrow. Are you going?" I ask.

"Yeah. Let's go together. There's a parade in Sukhbaatar Square tomorrow morning at around nine, and then the opening ceremony is in the stadium at around eleven." John withdraws a piece of paper from his back pocket. It's an English-language schedule of events for Naadam. He points to an entry midway down the page and laughs. "Hey, there's going to be uncle-bone shooting at one o'clock." It's either a misprint or a very bad translation.

"Does that mean there going to shoot the bones of people's uncles?," I inquire sarcastically.

"It's a long-standing tradition in Mongolia that when you have kids, your brothers have to cut off a part of their body and donate their bones. That's why a lot of men kill their sisters when they get pregnant. Or they leave the country. It's tough being an uncle in Mongolia, especially around Naadam time." John keeps a straight face and takes the joke about as far as it could go. "Men tend to hate their nephews and nieces here."

The typographical error in the program was actually meant to announce the *ankle-bone* shooting competition. The official name for Naadam is "Eriin Gurvan Naadam," which is translated as the "Manly Three Sports." But there is a fourth competition that seems to be the not-so-manly little brother of the other games. It is ankle-bone shooting, and it draws a loyal and rowdy following. The competitions take place in a tent near the Naadam stadium, where men try to knock down rows of sheep ankles (which are surprisingly only the size of an acorn) by flicking another piece of bone with their middle finger. The shooter carefully balances a small, flat wooden board with a vertical guide rail on his knee as he crouches down and takes aim at the targets, about ten feet away. The competitors are studies in concentration, completely emotionless as, all along the edges of the shooting area, men sing and chant in wailing overtones. A direct hit gets a raucous cheer from the crowd, and then the chanting begins again with nephews and uncles alike joining in the lively chorus.

"I'll meet you in the guesthouse in the morning. I'd like to go see that parade, and then the opening ceremony and some wrestling," I tell John.

"So, no UB Palace then?"

"I've got some e-mail to catch up on. I'll see you in the morning. Thanks for the beers." I head back out into the streets in a slight haze and float down the sidewalk as if in a dream world. Ulaan Baatar, Mongolia isn't a place I ever thought I'd be grateful to be in. It's an ugly charmless city, to tell you the truth, but it suddenly feels like home here. I feel safe, secure. It's a haven of rest from the daily torture I've put myself through. It's a floating raft in the middle of a long ocean I'm swimming across. I needed this city to be here. I needed those two pints of Chinggis lager, and I needed to have a conversation. From here I'll have to decide if I can carry on with the expedition. But first, there's Naadam to watch.

According to most sources, Naadam competitions began in the twelfth century, although it should be said that there is very little written history of Mongolia before that time. They were annual gatherings where men would show off their prowess in wrestling, archery, and horsemanship, three important skills for a warrior on the central Asian steppe. In the twentieth century, when the Soviet-backed Communist Party was in power, the date of Naadam was fixed to July 11, in honor of the date of the People's Revolution, July 11, 1921. Today, it is a time of travel, family reunions, drinking, and of course viewing the events of the competition in person or on television.

The opening parade in Sukhbaatar Square used to be an extravaganza that, during Communist times, was filled with military and government personnel. Today, there's still a bit of pomp and circumstance, but the focus of the parade is the carrying of the Nine Yak Tails. These yak tails are adorned with colorful ribbons and propped onto tall poles. They represent the nine original clans that Genghis Khan united to begin the Great Mongol Empire, and they're carried by elaborately dressed horsemen into the Naadam stadium for the opening ceremony. I could have learned all this by actually watching the parade, but the fact is that John's little schedule of events had given the wrong time for the parade. It was at 7:00 A.M., not 9:00 A.M.

John and I walk aimlessly around an empty Sukhbaatar Square before we run into a Swedish tourist who was staying at our guesthouse. "Isn't there supposed to be a parade here?" John asks incredulously.

"You missed it. It was about two hours ago. Everyone is down at the stadium now." She gives us a coy smile as if to say, "You silly boys, you look so lost."

I'm kind of pissed off at John, but I'm just as much to blame for not doing my own fact-checking. "Do you know where the stadium

is?" I ask, inadvertently reinforcing her impression that we are
totally clueless.

"It's on the other side of Peace Bridge, just down that road over
there. I'm going right now. Do you wanna come?"

"Yeah, let's go," I reply quickly, happy to have some other company. John's been telling me how great the disco was last night and
how I should have been there. His meandering, pointless anecdotes
are grating on me this morning. And, he's wearing a cowboy hat
and leather vest along with a pair of Thai fisherman's trousers. He
looks incredibly ridiculous, although I'd score him a few points for
originality.

After marching about a mile down the road, we cross a bridge
and immediately I can see the stadium and the throngs of people
outside it. The stadium holds at least twenty thousand people, and
there are thousands more walking around its perimeter. We buy
tickets from a random middle-aged Mongolian guy standing outside the stadium and try to make our way inside. It takes an
extraordinary amount of pushing and squeezing just to get up the
stairs to the bleachers and another ten minutes worth of effort to
find places to sit. The opening ceremonies are under way.

We suffer in the hot sun through speeches and processions of
marching and horse-riding groups of children and adults, many
wearing traditional or historical costumes. Judging by the crowds in
the stadium, some people must find this interesting, but I can't tell
what the hell is going on or understand any of the speeches. I'm

most impressed when several parachutists tumble out of an airplane and float down into the grassy infield of the stadium, perfectly hitting the mark. The rest of it reminds me of an Olympic opening ceremony, but in a foreign language with no Hollywood-style special effects.

"You should be out there golfing, hitting targets with your three-iron," John blurts out. "I know some people. I might be able to arrange it for you." I tend to have a hard time telling whether John's being serious or sarcastic.

"I could try to pick off those guys on the horses as they ride around the track. I'd need a pitching wedge, though." I've assumed sarcastic.

"You could aim for the parachutists. Now, that would be good."

The Swedish woman, whose name I learn is Anna, glances at us but chooses not to get involved in the conversation. After a couple more minutes, I inform my companions that I'm going outside the stadium to see if I can get something to drink.

This, as it turns out, is where the real action is. There are hundreds of food stalls surrounding the stadium selling skewers of grilled mutton, plates of rice and stew, fried noodles, and of course *khuushuur*. Khushuur and the Naadam festival carry an important association, like popcorn and movies or hot dogs and baseball. Most translations call the khuushuur a mutton pancake, but that doesn't do justice to its greasiness. It's a deep-fried meat pastry filled with fatty mutton and onions. You'll be sure to cover your fingers, face, and esophagus with grease after a khuushuur feast. They only cost ten cents each, and they're extremely addictive to those with a proclivity for things greasy, like the majority of the Mongolian population. There are literally hundreds of thousands of khuushuur sold every year during Naadam.

Then there's *airag,* the traditional drink of Naadam. It's as unlikely a beverage as one could imagine as a country's national drink. Airag is fermented horse milk. The concept of milking horses is already way beyond most of our capacities already, but *fermented* horse milk? Could this be for real?

Yes, we're talking thousands of gallons real. By late June, there is enough grass for the foals to eat, and the mares can stop feeding them. What else is a nomadic herdsman to do but milk the horses and let the milk ferment into an alcoholic, bubbly, sour concoction, with some occasional mixing and churning to get the bacterial cultures really working? Airag, like yak-butter tea or camel cheese, is an acquired taste.

Along with sellers of khuushuur and airag, the area surrounding the stadium teems with strolling merchants plying souvenirs to tourists, television crews scanning the scene for a decent shot, and Korean missionaries seizing the opportunity to spread the word of Jesus. Many of the Mongolians are wearing their finest clothes, and families are having picnics on empty lots of bare ground within earshot of the stadium loudspeakers. It's a mad carnival, and everyone is having a great time. I stroll leisurely through it all, stopping for an occasional khuushuur or to take a photo. Eventually, I end up at the archery arena. It's not as crowded as the main stadium, and the grandstands are close enough to the archers for me to gain an extraordinary view of the action.

It's easy to imagine archery competitions going back thousands of years. Bows and arrows were important tools of warfare, and accuracy was paramount to their effectiveness. The legends of William Tell and Robin Hood romanticize the marksmanship of skilled archers, as do ancient tales from China, Japan, and many other cultures across the globe. One of the reasons that the Mongolian Empire stretched a quarter of the way around the world was because of the Mongolians' skill at archery and because of technological advancements in bow construction that allowed arrows to pierce their enemies' armor. I watch as several men wearing royal blue robes with orange sashes and traditional embroidered skullcaps with pointed tops draw back their bows in concentration. These are the descendants of Genghis Khan's great warriors, and they hold their bows comfortably, as if they were born to it. Considering twenty-first-century warfare, archery is only valuable as a sport now, but it's a sport that Mongolian culture takes very seriously.

The most serious sport of all, though, is wrestling. In the late afternoon, I wander back into the stadium and find it half empty. I scan the crowd for John's cowboy hat and Anna's white-blond hair, but they're nowhere to be seen. I settle into a front-row seat to watch the wrestling competition, which is in full swing. I understand the scarcity and the apathy of the audience when I learn that there are 512 wrestlers competing in nine rounds of single-elimination action. The early rounds feature bouts between relative unknowns or David and Goliath–style mismatches, because wrestlers get to choose their opponent based on a seeding system.

There's no confusion about this being a "manly" sport, because all the wrestlers are wearing Speedo briefs with tall curve-toed leather boots. They wear long-sleeved half-shirts that have no front, allegedly because once upon a time, a woman disguised herself as a man and won the competition, upsetting a great number of manly men. Some wrestlers' physiques are in the Hulk Hogan category with an intimidating muscular stature, and others are in the Fat Albert category with their strength hiding behind substantial bulk. But they all look strong. I wouldn't want to grapple with any of them, even if I didn't have to wear nut-hugging skivvies. Mongolian kids start wrestling as soon as they can stand, and the technique and strategy of wrestling are ingrained at an early age.

The rules of the matches are simple. Take your opponent down to the ground and you win. Period. I've heard of foreigners taking part in wrestling competitions in Mongolia. Guys who thought it looked easy—NCAA football players, high school state wrestling champs, and the like. They all gave it their best effort at one of the smaller Naadam competitions around the country. And they all got their asses kicked. It's not purely about strength or size, but about balance and technique and how to react to an opponent's tactic. By contrast, Mongolians do well when wrestling abroad. In Japan, where sumo wrestling is the national sport, the champion is a Mongolian.

By the time the finals are reached on the second day of competition, the stadium will again be packed solid and every television set in the entire country will be tuned in to the event. The winner receives national fame and respect and becomes a household name. Every boy in Mongolia dreams of being a national wrestling champion.

Becoming a champion jockey, on the other hand, is something that boys and girls can do right away. Naadam's third sport, horse-racing, is also a big draw and takes place in the open countryside, about twenty-five kilometers outside the city limits. There are several categories of races, but they are all of the long-distance cross-country variety, with the longest race totaling thirty kilometers. But the most surprising thing I learned was that all the jockeys in these national horse-racing competitions are boys and girls between the ages of five and ten. When I had been caught in the middle of the race a week ago in Baganuur, I had thought it was a special children's race. But, in fact, small children are the best choice to ride the racehorses because of their diminutive weight and stature. And most children in Mongolia learn to ride at an early age, so finding skilled jockeys is not a problem.

I ventured out to Khui Doloon Khudag to watch the racing on the second day of Naadam, July 12. The race site is uninhabited steppe

pastureland for most of the year, until a week before Naadam. Then
the trainers arrive and set up a small city of gers to prepare for the
races. Soon after, dozens more gers pop up in long rows where families will sell khuushuur and other foodstuffs to race fans. It's the carnival coming to town meets the Wild West. Horses gallop down the
lanes, kicking up dust while pedestrians try not to get trampled.
Foodsellers do just as much business with those on horseback as they
do with those on foot, and "ride-thru" transactions are not
uncommon. A haze of dust over this makeshift town almost blocks
out the sun, but somewhere among it all is the start/finish line. I
found my way there and began speaking with a smartly dressed
Mongolian man. He asked me about horse-racing in America.

"You have a big race, too, the Kentucky Derby, right?"

"Yes, that's correct. The Kentucky Derby is a big race in
America."

"Kentucky is a state?"

I answer affirmatively.

"And do the horses race across the state?"

"No," I laugh, "they race inside a stadium. Like the Naadam
stadium."

"Oh, and how many times do they go around?" He makes a cir-
cular motion with his finger to represent the horses going around.

I raise my own index finger in the air. "Once."

We both remain silent for moment. It's a moment for me to feel
culturally inferior, as if Crocodile Dundee said to me patronizingly:

"That's not a knife . . . *this* is a knife." But the Mongolian man just smiles casually as I force out an awkward laugh. The greatest horse race in America is one lap around a mile-and-a-quarter track. Total wagers on the race are more than one hundred million dollars. That's about two percent of Mongolia's gross domestic product. The whole event seems so contrived and false. Derby horses have to undergo pre-race tests now for performance-enhancing drugs. Mister Ed on steroids. How bizarre is that?

And meanwhile in this nation filled with perhaps the world's most skilled horsemen, five-year-old kids are riding bareback for thirty kilometers across the steppe in the country's most prestigious race. Some kids fall off their horses during the race and get seriously injured. Some horses make it to the homestretch and then collapse and die. There is no wagering and there are no drug tests. The jockeys who finish the race usually get rewarded with an ice-cream cone. It doesn't get any more real than this. No bullshit, no pretense. I am completely in awe of this spectacle.

I'm nudged out of my contemplation by the elbow of the Mongolian man. "Look," he says, pointing, "here they come."

The rising cloud of dust over the nearest hill in the distance brings back a feeling of déjà vu. I can't believe that I was actually golfing through the middle of a race course last week in Baganuur, with the region's best jockeys flying past me.

Several horses separate from the pack as they draw nearer to the finish line. It's clear that the horses are laboring to the finish, wanting to be done with the ordeal. The young rider in the lead frantically swings a rope, whacking the horse's rear flanks on the left side, then the right. The crowd around me stands and leans against the rope that separates the race fans from the race course, while police try to control them. My view of the finish line is obscured.

"Did the boy in yellow win?" I ask my neighbor.

"Yes, he finished first," the man says with a smile. "There is going to be a big crowd around him now. Everyone wants to get some of the sweat from the horse. If you can wipe some of the sweat from the winning horse on yourself, then you will have good luck for the next year."

It seems an odd custom, and quite frankly I'm not sure I'd rush to get in line to wipe the sweat from a horse's backside onto my head. Even if it did guarantee me good luck for a year. But it's a part of the history and culture of these people, and I can't help but feel inspired by the casual and unpretentious way they go about their business.

The thousands of foreign tourists who have come to watch the Naadam festival this year, myself included, will tell stories of the peculiar customs of the Mongolian people. But to the locals, we are the strange ones with our once-around-the-track horse races, our "professional" wrestlers, and our private property laws (not to mention strange obsessions with golf). Naadam has been going on for hundreds of years, and it will continue—with or without tourists.

Mongolia has again surprised me with its firm hold on tradition, even in a rapidly changing world. I'll never completely feel the significance of Naadam as the Mongolians do, but the sincerity and lack of pretense in its formal observations have led me to realize how fortunate I am to be a witness to it. I've got a long way to go and a lot to learn.

Sogoo's heavy frame comfortably weighs down the front seat of his jeep where he sits with the driver's door open. Like many of the truck drivers I've met in Mongolia, he's got strong forearms, well-worn hands, and a sizeable beer gut. It's more likely a mutton-and-vodka gut, but you get the picture.

Sogoo owns a light-gray UAZ-469 jeep, or *jaryus* in Mongolian (so named because *jaryus* means "69" in Mongolian, and the original model was a UAZ-69). Although Toyota and Mitsubishi SUVs are becoming more common on the streets of Ulaan Baatar, the Russian-made UAZ jeeps and vans are still the vehicles of choice when venturing into the countryside. They're cheap, rugged, and amazingly simple in their mechanics, an important feature since all automotive repairs are performed by the vehicle's driver wherever a breakdown occurs. Every Mongolian driver carries a toolbox and a spare bucket of miscellaneous nuts, bolts, and springs that can be used to resolve any mechanical problem with MacGyver-like efficiency. On the remote dirt roads of the countryside, any disabled vehicle will receive assistance from every passing truck or van. Mongolians never think twice about taking hours out of their day to assist someone in need. The act of driving past a broken-down car or truck without stopping is incomprehensible to them. These good Samaritan–like qualities are exercised often because these UAZ jeeps, while practical and inexpensive, don't go through a rigorous quality assurance program on the Russian assembly line. One Mongolian man told me that a jaryus isn't worthy until it's three or four years old. By then, everything has fallen apart and been repaired solidly by Mongolian drivers in the countryside.

Sogoo's jeep has a spider-crack on the passenger side of the windshield where someone has obviously smacked his head. Tiny longitudinal tendrils have begun to spread out across the rest of glass and, at a certain angle, they reflect the morning sunlight in a bright glare. I squint as I introduce myself and shake his hand.

"I'll get my things and then we'll be ready to go," I say to Sogoo.

I've spent the past week stressing out over how I could continue the expedition without killing myself. I rehashed all the ideas of camels, horses, and carts. I've considered solar-powered dune buggies, remote-control cars, and sidecar motorcycles. I've taken all the harebrained schemes and unsolicited advice from everyone I've spoken to during the past week and given serious consideration to everything. But only one idea made sense to me—hiring a man with a four-wheel-drive jeep to carry all the water, food, golf balls, and camping gear while I golf. When the owners of the guesthouse where I was staying offered to connect me with Sogoo, I jumped at the chance to get my expedition on the move again. Especially since my extended respite in the capital had begun to draw some skeptical responses from Ulaan Baatar's expatriate community.

"You're still here?" It's an all-too-common salutation that I've been receiving lately. This time it's Andy, an American in his twenties who works at the U.S. Embassy. He finds me sitting alone at an outdoor table at my favorite beer joint.

"I'm leaving tomorrow," I respond. "I found a guy with a jeep to come with me as far as Arvaikheer."

"Oh, so you're not going to walk any more?"

"No!" I answer, "No, no, no. I am still going to walk and golf, but he's going to carry all the stuff. I'll just meet him at the end of the day to eat dinner and set up camp and all that."

"Cool. You got yourself a caddy," Andy replies matter-of-factly. I've met Andy a couple of times before, and he's one of the few people who seems to understand exactly what I'm trying to accomplish. His comprehension no doubt stems from the fact that he's a golfer. He knows how difficult it is to hit a three-iron.

"Maybe I'll join you some time," Andy continues. "I've got some
vacation days built up. I could golf with you for a week or so. I'll
bring a couple of cases of beer with me."

"That seems like a fair cost for having the privilege of golfing
with me," I reply sarcastically. "Seriously, if you want to do it, we'll
have to plan out exactly where you want to meet. It's not as if I'll be
around many telephones out there." This idea of Andy meeting me
for a week of golf has me pretty excited. I'd have someone talk to
every night. We could have golf competitions. I'd actually cook real
food. And the beer . . . was he serious about the beer?

I'm pondering all the possibilities when I feel a slap on my back.
"Hey, you're still here?"

This time it's a young Canadian guy named Oz who's teaching
English at a local school. I've met him a few times before as well.
Ulaan Baatar has a small expat community, and it's easy to spot
familiar faces in its most popular restaurants and bars. In my previous travels, the foreigners I met were mostly fellow backpackers
with stories similar to mine. But Mongolia seems to attract those
who are seeking something a little less ordinary. There are volun-
teers from all over the world who are working in orphanages
around the city, trying to help with the problem of increasing numbers of homeless children that has gotten worse since the end of
communism and the dismantling of many of the social safety nets
that were in place. I've met people who are teaching Buddhism to
Buddhist Mongolians, an idea that sounds ludicrous at first but

begins to make sense in the context of the crackdown on religion that took place during the Communist rule.

Even the temporary visitors to the country seem more interesting. I've met several amateur adventurers who have completed horse-riding or mountain-biking expeditions around the country. In the guest house, I've met odd birds like John the Canadian (who suddenly disappeared about three days ago and is presumably chasing his horse somewhere near the Russian border by now) and Leo, a dreadlocked Australian in his thirties whose sole aim is to capture enough footage with his video camera to make an original documentary. In a way, this peculiar conglomeration of misfits and visionaries makes me feel more comfortable here. No one I've met really seems shocked by my adventure. Amused, yes, but shocked, no.

Amusement is not the reaction I expect from Sogoo, however, when I tell him that he should wait while I grab my gear. As he stares at me with a quizzical expression, I reach a rapid conclusion—he doesn't speak English. My initial excitement about resuming the expedition with a new acquaintance becomes slightly dulled with this discovery. I won't be having long conversations about the meaning of life with Sogoo any time soon. No swapping mutton recipes or debating Nietzsche. I resign myself to this disappointing news by assuming that at least he'll be able to understand what I'm doing and what I expect from him. This should be enough.

A few hours later, I realize that this is not the case. At the outskirts of the industrial zone of Ulaan Baatar, I ask Sogoo to stop the jeep near the top of a hill. It's not far from where the Naadam horse racing took place, and I know that only open steppe lies ahead to the west. I grab my three-iron and a small daypack that I've filled with spare golf balls, a water bottle, and a few snacks. I walk about a hundred meters from the road, tee the ball up, take a few practice swings, and then launch a Pinnacle golf ball up into the blue sky. The ball hits the downslope of the hill and rolls an extra fifty yards. It's a good way to begin the hole, and I set off again across the grass, counting my steps as I've done thousands of times already. It feels good to be golfing again.

After my second shot, Sogoo comes barreling across the grass in his jeep and pulls up next to me. He looks concerned and, after turning off the ignition, he starts on a barrage of questions that I can only partially understand.

"I walk. I walk here," I say to him while pointing to the long valley ahead. "You, road, there. You, five kilometers. You and I, five kilometers," I continue in my best Mongolian. I bring my hands together as I say the "you, I, five kilometers" bit, and Sogoo gives a nodding affirmation. He says a couple more sentences that I can't understand and then I repeat "you, I, five kilometers." We both look at each other and nod several times as if we had just made a complex military invasion strategy. I feel like if I were to say, "You don't understand a darn word that I just said, do you?" that he would continue nodding conclusively. I resist the urge and return to optimism.

"Okay?" I ask.

"Okay."

When I decided to hire a driver, I was worried that he would be extremely unsatisfied with the job. Drivers like to drive. I was asking him to drive for two minutes, stop for two hours, and then drive for another two minutes, and so on. It's got to be boring. Sure, it's an easy job, but the days are going to pass very slowly. I knew it would take exactly the right man for the job. And this morning, when I learned that he didn't speak any English, an additional worry about communication arose. Our little rendezvous plan will be the first test of our multilingual (or nonlingual) rapport.

Five kilometers and thirty-five shots later, I get my answer. Sogoo's gray jeep is parked directly ahead of me, easily visible on the top of a hill. It is also parked next to a ger, not far from the road. I continue with a few more shots until I reach the ger and then bashfully poke my head inside the door.

Sogoo calls my name and motions for me to come in. He grabs a small wooden stool and slaps it with his hand, directing me to sit. There is an older couple in the ger, and the woman cooks over the central stove while the man chats to Sogoo and draws slowly from a hand-rolled cigarette. I instantly feel at home and simultaneously relieved that Sogoo is the kind of man who can easily talk with strangers. My lack of communication skills won't be much of a problem, because he can break the ice and do most of the talking with the locals that we'll meet, like this old couple.

The old man leans over and pours me a bowl of hot milk tea from an aluminum kettle; and as he does so, he lets out an enormous fart. No one flinches. It's not the first time I've witnessed an indiscriminate display of flatulence in Mongolia. People have farted in midconversation, while introducing themselves, or during periods of complete silence inside a ger. It never seems to cross their minds that there is anything wrong with this. And, I'd have to agree that, in the overall importance of life's concerns, there isn't. People have to fart, plain and simple. I've even taken to the habit of letting one rip whenever I feel the need myself. It's liberating not to be bound by the restrictive social norms of the society where I was brought up. My only worry is that I'll become all too accustomed to this and find myself a year from now in a room full of engineers, passing gas while giving a PowerPoint presentation. It may not be the best way to impress potential clients.

As I take a sip of the lactose-rich milk tea that I'm offered, a young man steps through the door and sits on one of the two beds next to the old man. I assume that he's the son or son-in-law of this couple. The old woman must have been waiting for his arrival, because as soon as he sits down, she lifts the lid on the pot she's been watching and begins removing pieces of meat and placing them into a plastic basin. When the basin is placed on the floor in front of Sogoo and me, I realize that it's not filled with meat per se, but with animal innards. Long coils of beige intestines and several slabs of brown and coffee-colored organs sit steaming in a huddled mass.

Sogoo removes a knife from his pocket and slices off a chunk of the liver. He turns to me and, with his open palms pointing to the bucket, invites me to dig in. My Swiss Army knife isn't as manly as the other men's knives, but its hardened steel blade easily carves off a section of intestine. I'm surprised at the complexity of its rich flavor and generally impressed, except for the slight aftertaste of partially chewed grass.

As the old man, and then finally the younger man, take their turns at the cooked organs, I frantically try to remember the lessons from my tenth-grade biology class. I think I can identify the kidneys, and maybe the stomach, but I can't successfully find a match for the spleen, duodenum, and heart. I'm not even sure if a sheep has a duodenum, but I'm pretty sure the white blobby mass that Sogoo is digging into is the brain. Like a true connoisseur, he casually slices off a slab of liver, smears some of the brain matter on top, and pops the whole thing into his mouth. I figure that this may be the only opportunity in my life to savor that unique combination of internal organs, so I reach over and copy Sogoo's exact moves. The contrast in textures melds the two substances perfectly into one delectable bite. With a garlic-butter sauce to accompany it, it's easy to imagine sharing this meal with Jacques Pépin over a bottle of Côtes du Rhône.

As it is, sharing this gastronomical adventure with Sogoo has given me a new appreciation of his services. His skills as an ambassador will likely introduce me to dozens more families and the intimate goings-on of their lives, insights into Mongolian life that I could never experience without him. Several other benefits have already become obvious.

From a safety perspective, I couldn't do much better than to have a Mongolian man watch out for me all day and park his jeep next to my tent every night. I've never felt in danger at any time, but I've had enough confrontations with snarling dogs and angry yaks to appreciate the presence of another human in my camp. Additionally, after several Mongolians told me that I was fortunate to make it so far without being robbed or harassed while walking alone in the countryside, I've become less complacent about security issues. Sure, these were "city" Mongolians who told me this, and it ran contrary to all my experiences of generous hospitality; but, nevertheless, it'd be foolhardy to assume that I know more about their country than they do.

Another advantage is the drastic change in my food and water consumption. I bought two twenty-liter plastic jugs in Ulaan Baatar that we'll keep filled with water. Today, I've already drunk a liter and a half of water during my first half-day of golfing. This is a huge change from the days when I rationed every drop and often stretched a liter and a half to last all day, perpetually worrying about where my next refill would come from. Back in Khentii Province, I had to detour several times to pass by a ger where I could ask for water. Most gers I visited had one or two barrels just outside the door and, after some bewildered looks and monosyllabic small talk, I usually managed to impose enough to get my bottles refilled. I never knew exactly where this water came from, but I never asked, preferring to ignorantly quench my thirst rather than add water-borne diseases to my list of worries.

Along with the addition of the water jugs to my equipment, we also stopped at one of the city's markets on the way out of town and stocked up on potatoes, onions, cabbage, and lots of canned meat and fish. The box of provisions that we tossed into the backseat of the jeep must have weighed sixty pounds. My overexuberant food purchases were akin to the Skipper from Gilligan's Island bingeing at Denny's on his first day back on the mainland. I was determined to replenish some of the body mass I'd lost in the past two months.

The most important aspect to Sogoo's presence, though, is the fact that I'm actually enjoying golf again. Without the burden of pushing my cart or lifting my pack on and off my back after every shot, I can concentrate on my golf skills and actually take pleasure in swinging the club 150 times a day. Golf, an enjoyable pastime for most of my life, had become nothing more than a necessary task, a loathsome physical responsibility that made my miserable days even more unenjoyable. The realization of this seems even more ludicrous, given the fact that this is a *golf* expedition. Acquiring a caddy is one of the smartest moves I've made yet.

With a belly full of sheep organs, I bid the family good-bye and resume the day's golf. Clouds of locusts and butterflies scatter as I tromp through the grass and tee up the next shot. I look over to see Sogoo and the young man looking under the hood of Sogoo's jeep.

"The jeep's okay?," I ask.

Sogoo gives me a smile. "Okay."

"Okay," I answer, and I smile back. This should be fun.

A ndré!"

I can barely hear my name being called through the deafening wind whipping across the steppe, but I recognize the distinctive Australian accent.

"You've made some good progress, mate."

It's the voice of Leo, the amateur videographer who I'd met in the guesthouse in Ulaan Baatar several days ago. He had mentioned that he and Anders, a young Danish guy also staying in the guesthouse, were interested in joining me for a few days and filming a portion of my golf adventure. I was thrilled with the interest that he showed, but I had doubted he would ever make it.

The first and most obvious problem was that he didn't have a vehicle or a cell phone, and I'd be in the middle of a random field hitting a golf ball.

"I can't guarantee that I'll be near the main road," I had warned him.

"That's all right, we'll get on a public minibus and keep an eye out for you. Don't worry, we'll find you."

It's the kind of plan that normally gets made at 2 A.M., after a night of heavy drinking—full of good intentions but weak on the follow-through. I'm completely astonished that they actually attempted it, and succeeded.

"We saw the reflection of the sun shining from your golf club," Anders says in an amused tone of voice as he and Leo approach me. "The driver of the van didn't want to stop. He kept trying to tell us that we were stopping in the wrong place."

I imagine Leo and Anders, who know about five words in Mongolian between them, trying to convince a vanload of Mongolians that they wanted to get out at this random point along the road.

"I'm sure the locals were amused," I reply. "You guys don't know how lucky you are to find me. This is the closest I've been to the road all day. This morning, I golfed across that ridge back there." I turn and point back to a hilltop that is nearly a kilometer away from the road. "I just can't believe this. Well, welcome to Golf Mongolia."

By this time, Leo has withdrawn his video camera from its bag.

A tiny beep emanates from the camera as he pans slowly around, capturing 360 degrees of Mongolian steppe before stopping with the lens pointing directly at my face.

"So, André, can you tell us where we are now?"

"You don't waste any time, do you?," I respond before clearing my throat and assuming a narrative tone. "We're in Töv aimag, about seventy-five miles west of Ulaan Baatar; but more important, this is hole number seven of the Golf Mongolia Expedition."

"And how's it going today?"

"Today, the wind is the big challenge. It's blowing directly at me at about twenty kilometers per hour."

I explain the strategy of hitting the ball on a low trajectory, a technique used by golfers when hitting into a stiff wind. As Leo keeps the camera rolling, I demonstrate the adjustments to the swing that are necessary. Finally, I approach the golf ball and prepare to hit it.

"Let's see what you can do, André," Leo encourages while kneeling down in the grass and focusing in on the ball. This is the most pressure I've felt since my first shot of the expedition back in Choibalsan when Alain was watching. But Alain wasn't a golfer, nor did he have a video camera. This footage is likely to be viewed by other golfers who could critique my swing. *"That hacker golfed across Mongolia?"* I can hear them say. Looking good has never been a priority of mine. The shoulders of my blue T-shirt are discolored where I've been wiping the sweat and dust from my forehead for the past three days, and my khaki shorts

are covered with black soot from my camping stove. Nevertheless, the leering and critical eye of the camera evokes an elevated
sense of vanity. I execute what I imagine to be the perfect golf
swing.

"Wow, that's a good shot, man!" Anders shouts.

I breathe a sigh of relief. My first filmed golf shot of the expedition was a good one. That'll make the final edit of Leo's documentary for sure, I imagine, if he ever gets around to making one. Leo's
presence with his video camera has given me a renewed sense of
confidence. Someone actually cares about my expedition. Someone
is actually *filming* it. I've got two witnesses now who can see the difficulties that I have to overcome. They'll see the terrain and feel the
force of the wind and the intensity of the sun. They'll know what
it's like to camp on the steppe and cook simple meals over a tiny
cookstove. And they'll understand the pleasure and the difficulty of
walking twenty-five kilometers across the steppe every day.

After walking 185 steps, I drop my small backpack to the
ground and begin searching for my ball. With the pack as a refer-
ence point, I walk in gradually increasing concentric circles and
sweep my three-iron through the tall grass like a scavenger
sweeping a metal detector across a beach. But after five minutes, no
treasure is found.

"I guess that one's lost," I say to Leo and the camera, throwing
my hands up in frustration. It's the seventh golf ball I've lost today,
but the fourth in the last hour. This particular valley is filled with

tall weeds that reach almost as high as my knees. The weeds shimmer in the sunlight as the wind blows across this sea of green. It's beautiful, but absolutely crap for golf.

I reach into my backpack and retrieve my GPS receiver along with another golf ball.

"What are you doing now, André?" Leo asks while holding the camera up to his right eye.

"I'm marking the coordinates," I answer. "That was a sponsored ball."

"How many sponsors have you got?"

"Not nearly enough," I answer. "But all of my sponsors get one golf ball that I write their name on and play in their honor. When I lose the ball, I'll mark the coordinates on my GPS receiver and then put the data on my Web site."

I line up my next shot and stroke a low-flying drive into the stiff breeze. My golf game is solid, but concerns over the terrain are steadily mounting. As Leo and Anders walk with me, I lose three more balls in the next two hours. After my 143rd shot, I call it a day and we set up camp near the top of a ridge. Leo and Anders are sharing a tent—or, rather, miscellaneous parts of several tents— that they borrowed from the guest house. With some help from Sogoo, they manage to assemble enough poles and ropes to keep the A-frame nylon structure from sagging too dramatically. Assembling my modern expedition-designed tent next to theirs has the effect of driving a Mercedes onto a lot full of UAZ jeeps. But they seem happy just to be here in the open natural grasslands, far from the gritty congestion of Ulaan Baatar.

The presence of Leo and Anders brought episodes of levity, hilarity, and genuine enjoyment to the next three days and nights of my expedition. Episodes such as Anders's rescue of a sheep with a broken leg from a mountaintop, a sheep that he carried three kilometers on his shoulders despite the sarcastic comments from Leo and me that the Mongolians he brought it to would just slaughter it and eat it anyway. But the fun masked a growing concern for me that gave serious doubt to the continued success of the expedition. With increasing frequency, I was passing through regions of the country where the short fairwaylike grass was being replaced by a flood of tall savannah-like weeds that swallowed up my golf balls with astounding voracity.

The small town of Lun marked the end of my seventh hole, and also brought the departure of Leo and Anders. After a night of torrential rain, the soaked pair packed up their permeable makeshift tent and returned by public transportation to the capital city. The sadness of their departure was soon replaced, however, with feelings of dread and futility as I crossed the Tuul River and began a long ascent across rugged, hilly terrain covered in thick, lush vegetation. My battles against the dense army of weeds were just beginning. Where I had hoped for relief, only further exasperation awaited.

The summer of 2003 has brought an extraordinary amount of

rain, more than 50 percent above average, in some of the areas where my course leads me. While I was in Ulaan Baatar just after Naadam, one rain- and hailstorm became so severe that it caused flash flooding that was responsible for the deaths of fifteen people and left thirty families homeless. Storms like this in July are not unheard-of, as the bulk of Mongolia's precipitation falls in the summer months, but the frequency and intensity of the storms have been abnormal. For several consecutive evenings, I've had to batten down the hatches on my little tent and weather copious amounts of rainfall. But aside from me and the unfortunate individuals who were adversely affected by the flash floods, everyone is happy about this.

A rainy day in Mongolia is a good day. Rain brings smiles to the faces of local herders the way a Christmas Eve snowfall would delight Bing Crosby. In a land where the population depends so heavily on the health of its grazing livestock, rain ensures that the vegetation will be thick and plentiful—the precise reason why a cross-country golfer would be disheartened. As I continue from Töv Province into Övörkhangai Province, the calendar flips from July to August and nightly rainstorms become routine. I can almost hear the growth of the grass around my tent. On holes eight and nine, I have several days where I lose more than a dozen golf balls, an event that had not occurred in the first seven hundred kilometers of the expedition.

At times, I feel like I'm wading across the country rather than

walking. Getting through the initial aches and pains of the first few
weeks of the expedition was difficult. Coping with solitude and
mental angst in the next few weeks was equally difficult. But I
knew deep down that if I harnessed all my will and inner strength,
I could get through those difficulties. This obstacle is much different. This is a real, logistical challenge to the fundamentals of the
expedition. If I can't swing a club in the knee-high vegetation, or if
I can't find the ball after each shot, then it's just physically impossible to golf across Mongolia. Both of these are becoming certainties
with each passing day. I've tried to cope by playing on the slopes of
mountains rather than through the valleys, but even that terrain has
its challenges. Golfing across rock outcroppings isn't exactly an
improvement, or a long-term solution.

It's hard to show my frustration when everyone I meet is so
gleeful about the rain. Each time I enter a ger and meet a new
nomadic family, the conversation always starts off with a commen-
tary about the weather and how nicely the animals are fattening up
for winter. Even if I knew how to explain my predicament of
golfing difficulties in Mongolian, I wouldn't dare disturb the joyous
mood of the conversation with anything remotely negative, just as I
wouldn't ever say, "Hey, Bing, I know it's a White Christmas and
all, but who's going to shovel the damn driveway?"

Instead, I enjoy the positive aspects of the climatic predicament.
The plump green weeds get digested by goats, sheep, horses, and
cows, and the animals produce a cornucopia of dairy products.

Fresh yogurt and sour cheeselike loaves are found in every family's home. But in this neck of the steppe, there is one dairy product that makes a Mongolian's mouth water like no other—airag. I learn that airag is not just a Naadam beverage, but also a delectable drink to be enjoyed all summer long, especially in the weeks when the summer rains have given the millions of horses in Mongolia ripe foliage to ingest.

It's almost obsessive how they drink airag here. Large bowls of the stuff are ladled out, and one man drinks an entire bowl in less than a minute and then passes it back to the server. In one sitting, it is normal for someone to drink nearly a gallon of airag. If a slight lactose intolerance weren't enough, then the native bacteria swarming throughout the fermented milk are surely enough to give a jolt to anyone's digestive system. Without being too graphic, I'll just say that I experienced firsthand just how quickly the cycle of nutrient matter gets returned to the steppe from whence it originated.

But I'd be remiss if I didn't partake in the milk-drinking rituals of my host country; and, after several sittings, I actually began to enjoy the stuff. Sogoo is mad about it. Every evening, he uses my binoculars to search for gers that have mares tied up nearby, the telltale sign of the presence of airag. And every evening he looks at me with a hopeful expression and asks innocently, "What do you think, André? Should we go pay a visit to that ger over there?" How could I say no?

One of the basic lessons of airag consumption is that you have to
blow on the surface of the liquid as you bring it to your mouth. This
keeps all the bits of grass, dead insects, and crusted pieces of froth
that have accumulated on the sides of the fermentation barrel away
from your lips as you drink it. Fortunately, it's not impolite to leave
these in the bottom of the bowl when you hand it back.

My newfound love of horse milk aside, the final days of Hole
Nine are dominated by feelings of dread. Sogoo has informed me
that he won't be able to accompany me any further to the west
because he begins work at a school in Ulaan Baatar in two weeks.
I'll have to find a new caddy, unless I decide to proceed on my
own from Arvaikheer. Coupled with the uncertainty of whether
the terrain will allow me to continue, this option looks decidedly
unappealing, especially after the benefits of a hired caddy have
become so evident. In my long hours of solitude searching for
golf balls concealed in the heavy rough of Mongolia's fairways,
one thought has repeatedly crept into my distraught mind,
nestling amongst my doubts and fears—I won't be able to finish
the expedition.

This thought festers and grows like an infectious plague. The
healing powers of optimism keep it at bay until, at the outskirts of
Arvaikheer, we visit a local family who has built their ger near the
Ongi River. An old woman sits on a bed to the right of the doorway
and sews a *deel* made of bright purple fabric while a second,
younger woman tends to a pot of Mongolian milk tea over the

stove. I take a seat on the floor between Sogoo and an older man with a few wispy gray hairs poking out of his chin. He reaches his hand into the folds of his long woolen *deel,* just above the waist sash, and withdraws a small jade bottle and offers it to me with an open palm. I accept it with the open palm of my right hand and remove the ornate coral top, which is attached to a piece of metal that looks like half of a pair of tweezers. I know from experience that this is a snuff bottle, and I've read that the tradition of sharing snuff is a ritual greeting between men that goes back hundreds of years. This is my first opportunity to try it.

I dab a pinch of the finely ground tobacco onto my finger and inhale. The burning in my nostrils begins immediately, and my eyes begin to water as if I had just eaten a teaspoon of wasabi. A few seconds later, I'm sneezing uncontrollably. This gets an enormous laugh from the three Mongolians, and once again I find myself playing the familiar role of foreign entertainer. It's a role I don't mind, since it never fails to instantly endear me to the locals, and the mood and conversation are lightened.

Addressing the old man, whose face is adorned with the wrinkles of ageless wisdom, I try to ask in single words and broken phrases if he knows about the conditions of the grass in the next province, Bayankhongor. Sogoo catches the drift of my question and rephrases it to the three residents. The old man begins to respond, but I struggle to understand his meaning until he slowly reaches out with his arm and holds it steady, about one meter off the floor. The gesture confirms my worst fears. Sure, the airag is flowing freely in Bayankhongor Province, but things look bad for golf.

In the most excruciating decision I've ever had to make, I decide to throw in the towel on Golf Mongolia 2003. I've completed exactly half of the expedition, and my experiences have given me valuable lessons on golf and life. But the final nine holes will have to wait until I'm a year older, and a year wiser.

W elcome back!" shouts Andy from across the restaurant. It's May 2004. Andy pulls a chair up to the table and joins me and several backpackers who are swilling pints of the local lager. "So, how does it feel to be back?" he asks.

This is my first full day in Mongolia in 2004. I arrived this morning by train via Russia.

"It's like being home again," I say, raising my glass in a toast to Mongolia. "Especially after being in Russia for the past four days. I almost cried for joy when I crossed the border this morning."

My dislike of Mongolia's northern neighbor is based on personal experience. I've got nothing against its people; I've met lots of Russians who are great people. But I've had enough unpleasant experiences within that country's borders to adamantly declare that I'll never set foot on Russian soil again. My first bad trip occurred in 2001. I had just arrived in St. Petersburg on a bus from Estonia; with some luck, I found my way from the bus station to a Metro stop. Only in the country for a matter of minutes, I labored to read the Cyrillic alphabet on the Metro map and recall what Russian words I could from the elementary Russian classes I had taken fourteen years earlier. I didn't get past the first word before I was whisked away into a jail cell by two policemen who proceeded to search all my belongings and interrogate me for unknown offenses. Although I wasn't shocked to discover that this could happen in Russia, I was surprised with the rapidity of my involvement in it. In the country for less than five minutes and I'm in jail. That has to be some kind of record.

All of my documents were in order and this was clearly a shakedown, a way to get a substantial sum of money from a frightened foreign tourist into the pockets of the policemen. I was resolute and assertive in my refusal to give them anything, and I'm fairly certain I got most of my money and belongings back before they finally caved in and let me go.

Later that day, I told the story to a Russian woman I met in a café to get her take on it. "This is normal," she said, "The police are allowed to take you into jail for a maximum of one hour with no reason. It sounds like the policemen were very friendly to you."

I was uneasy about the way "normal" and "friendly" seemed to be defined in Russia; so, to avoid any such problems on my second pass through this country, I booked myself a direct train ticket from Helsinki to Ulaan Baatar in the spring of 2004 for my return to Mongolia's final nine holes of golf. This travel plan only required a transit visa for Russia and one change of trains at Moscow's Yaroslavsky train station. But this ten-hour layover in Moscow turned out to be enough for Moscow's finest to get a second crack at me.

Just before the Mongolia-bound train was ready for departure, a police officer approached me and demanded to see my passport. As I was opening the page with my Russian visa, he ripped the passport from my hands and began to walk away. I followed him down a flight of stairs into the basement of the station and into a dimly lit concrete room where two other officers sat. They asked me to remove my backpack; and while two of them emptied it of its contents, another burly man pushed me up against a wall, patted me down, and took my money belt from around my waist. I protested as vehemently as I dared, but a quick assessment of the situation led me to one conclusion—I was screwed. They relieved me of several hundred dollars in various currencies and a small compass that I had been using to navigate around Mongolia, and then told me to take the rest of my belongings and get out of there. There's no sensation quite like being robbed by the police in a foreign country. Your options are few, and recourse is nonexistent. This was compounded by the facts that my train was leaving in twenty minutes and I had had experience with the "one-hour rule" previously.

Through a direct and calm appeal to the man who looked to be in charge, basically by saying the word "please" in Russian over and over, I managed to get half my money back, which he "found" under some papers on his desk. My persistent pleadings also got my compass returned; but when the big brawny guy took a step closer to me and started yelling, I knew it was time to make a quick exit. Diplomacy has its limits.

I recount the unfortunate tale for Andy and the small crowd around me and reiterate just how happy I am to be in Mongolia.

"When we crossed the border at Sukhbaatar, a Mongolian girl was selling *buuz* in one of those insulated canisters. I bought, like, ten of them. It felt so good to be eating mutton while getting my passport stamped. I was officially back." This gets a laugh from the crowd.

"That really sucks," Andy adds sympathetically. "Well, at least your three-iron is safe. I've still got it in my closet. I hope you don't mind, but I hit a bunch of your golf balls out into a field during the winter."

"No worries, I brought another two hundred with me," I answer. Andy had become a good friend of mine when I returned to Ulaan Baatar last year after postponing the conclusion of the expedition until 2004. In the three months that I spent in the capital, we played golf several times on Mongolia's only golf course, a "rustic" nine-hole set of links that was in its first year of operation. When I finally left the country last November, he offered to store my golf clubs, a cache of golf balls, and other expedition supplies for me over the winter. Upon my return this year, he's letting me stay in his apartment for a couple weeks while I prepare for the conclusion of my journey.

"How was the winter?" he asks.

"Well, let's see. When I left here I went to Beijing, Los Angeles, New Hampshire, London, and then Helsinki. You know, I was trying to keep up my nomadic lifestyle."

"How's Aino doing?" he asks at the mention of Helsinki. Aino is a Finnish woman with whom I shared an apartment in Ulaan Baatar last autumn. We had originally met in China in 2001, and we kept in touch over the next two years by e-mail. As fate would have it, she had received a grant to come to Mongolia to conduct research for her master's thesis for the second half of 2003. It didn't take long for us to rekindle our relationship, and my stopover in Finland was not just a practical way to exit Europe's easternmost border and return to Asia by train, but a purposeful visit to meet her family and see her homeland.

"She's doing great. Finland is a pretty cool place. I had an experience where, in the span of two minutes, I was both the hottest and the coldest I've ever been in my life."

"The famous Finnish sauna?"

"Yeah. Her family took me into this public sauna where the

temperature was two hundred and thirty degrees Fahrenheit. No bullshitting, I'm serious! The temperature was actually two hundred and thirty degrees. And right outside the door was a frozen lake where they had kept a hole open in the ice."

"Did you go in?"

"Dude, there were eighty-year-old women going in the water. Aino went in. Her mother went in! How could I *not* go in? I'm lucky I've got a strong heart, or I never would have made it back here."

"Every Finnish person I've met has been tough," Andy replies. "I think that's how they weed out the weaklings."

"By the way," he continues, "a guy who I work with at the embassy said that there's a *New York Times* reporter coming to Mongolia and that he was asking about you."

"No shit?"

"I told him you'd be staying with me when you got here, so it should be pretty easy to hook up with him. Good news, huh?"

It's great news, as a matter of fact. I had sent out another round of press releases announcing my return to Mongolia and the imminent conclusion to an epic adventure, but I hadn't received a very robust response. As far as media opportunities go, interest from the *New York Times* is about as good as it gets.

Over the next few days, I begin preparations for the expedition. My plan is to return to Arvaikheer the following week and proceed from the point where I left off last year. My top priority is finding a caddy who will accompany me for the remaining thousand kilometers and two months of golf. My first call is to Sogoo's cell phone. It's the only contact information I have for him, and it's been disconnected.

I receive more bad news when I stop by the guest house where they had introduced me to Sogoo. They tell me that they don't know how to get in touch with him and that the possibility of finding anyone else who would be willing to go with me for such a long time is doubtful. I spend the next week contacting every Mongolian person I know and asking if they know of anyone with a jeep who is available. The responses are all negative.

A few days later, I finally meet Jim Brooke, a reporter based out of the *Times*'s Tokyo office. As we sip coffee in the restaurant of the Puma Imperial Hotel, I relay my difficulties in finding an available driver. "I'd like to leave Ulaan Baatar this week," I explain, "but I can't find a caddy."

"I'm only in town for a few days," he responds. "There's a photographer coming from Korea, and we're going to work on several stories. If the timing works out, I'd like to go with you and watch you golf for a day or two. You'd have to leave by Friday to make this work, though."

My anxiety builds as I contemplate missing this incredible PR opportunity. Then Jim offers a suggestion. "There's a guy here who is arranging my transportation, named Chinzorig. Here's his phone number. Maybe he can help you out."

Immediately after the interview is finished, I rush back to Andy's apartment and give Chinzorig a call. "So, how long exactly will you need someone to be with you?" he asks in perfect English.

"At least fifty to sixty days," I answer.

"Wow, that's a long time, but let me see what I can do. I've got one guy in mind. He doesn't speak English, though."

"Zugeer, Bi jaakhan Mongol khel meden," I respond in passable Mongolian, telling Chinzorig that it's "no problem, I speak a little Mongolian."

While living in Ulaan Baatar last autumn, I took daily Mongolian language lessons for several weeks. With the possible exception of the click-and-whistle Pygmy languages, Mongolian is one of the most complicated and daunting languages to learn. The grammatical structure is completely foreign to speakers of any Indo-European language and includes eight cases—eight different forms of a word, depending on its context.

Spoken Mongolian is a nightmare. Even after learning to read and write simple sentences, I still had a hard time comprehending what any Mongolian person said to me. Imagine you're about to spit and then breathe in while trying to pronounce the letter k. That could mean about three different things depending on how much phlegm is in your throat.

The way to say "Mongolian language" in Mongolian is "Mongol khel," with a soft, aspirated k. It didn't take long for me and other foreign students to begin calling our language lessons "Mongol

Hell." But I stuck with them and, as a consequence, I can get by pretty well this year.

I hear Chinzorig chuckle softly on the other end of the phone when he hears my Mongolian. "That's great," he continues in English. "I'll give you a call to confirm, but let's plan on meeting tomorrow in front of the Puma Hotel."

I hang up the phone and pump my fist in the air with excitement. The greatest hurdle has been overcome. After spending the last few days purchasing maps, spare batteries, and other odds and ends, securing a caddy was the final piece of the puzzle. Now I just need to prepare myself mentally for golfing the remaining thousand kilometers across the western half of Mongolia.

"How have you prepared yourself for the second half of your expedition?" Jim asks me during the eight-hour drive from Ulaan Baatar to Arvaikheer.

"Well, I, umm . . . I did a lot of walking over the winter," I respond. "And I put on a few pounds in anticipation of losing a lot of weight this year." The last part of the answer is 100 percent true, while the first part is a slightly revised recollection of history. I didn't really do much to prepare, but I prefer to present myself more as an international adventurer than a cheeseburger-eating slacker, even if that means stretching the truth a bit. "A lot of walking" is a relative term. While I certainly exercised more than the average American, my fitness routine was not exactly that of a world-class athlete.

"Can you explain the reason why you didn't finish the expedition last year?" Jim continues.

I give him all the details about the extensive rainfall that occurred last summer and the subsequent explosion of weed growth that took place in July and August.

"So this is a race against time, in a way," he paraphrases, and looks at me for confirmation.

"Exactly. I've got to finish before the summer rains come in July. I learned my lesson last year. All this land right here," I continue, pointing out the window to a valley I struggled through last year, "all of this area was filled with lush green weeds that were knee-high." A glance out the window reveals a barren, brown landscape of shriveled dry grass. This is perfect golf terrain, and I feel the adrenaline surge as I anticipate my return to this natural golf course. A few hours later, the moment arrives.

For the first time in nine months, I'm swinging my three-iron in the open steppe of Mongolia. The club's grip has worn-down patches where my thumbs and fingers have held it thousands of times before, and my hands slide easily into their natural position. Hitting this club is like taking a walk with an old friend. Its familiarity and reliability comfort me and provide a measure of stability in an otherwise uncertain adventure. After an hour of golf, I haven't hit one bad shot.

I played golf only once after leaving Mongolia last November, and that was while visiting a friend in London just a month and a half ago. Playing at his local course, I hit my second shot onto the green on a par-five. He looked across fairway and called over to me: "Was that a three-iron you hit?"

"What else?" I answered. "I don't need all these other clubs in my bag."

It's ironic that I've fallen in love with this particular club. The three-iron is like British cuisine or the weather in Minnesota; no one would ever seriously declare that they enjoy it. Most golfers would prefer never to use it. But after six thousand swings with this baby, I might just be willing to sit down to a plate of mushy peas on a December morning in Duluth. My three-iron has become my favorite club.

I fall easily back into the routines I had adopted last year. I hit the ball and, while following its trajectory, squat down and lay my three-iron on the ground to mark its path. Then I swing my backpack up onto my shoulders and begin walking, counting my steps as I go. I even remember all the numerological aids that helped me keep track of my score. After my fourth shot, I think of Bobby Orr, the hockey player who wore the number 4 on his uniform for the Boston Bruins. I golf past a flock of sheep that grazes peacefully on the new sprouts of grass that poke up through the dry brown mass of last year's vegetation. I feel a connection with these animals, who, for long stretches of my expedition, represented the only other living mammals in sight. The sheep and goats especially have seen more of my golf swings than anyone else. They form the gallery of spectators lining the fairways of my course.

As I discuss the pleasures and pitfalls of "natural" golf with Jim, and pose for original photo ops in the vast but serene Mongolian landscape for the photographer, Jae, all doubts are erased about my decision to postpone the completion of the expedition until this year. It was the right choice.

By the end of my first full day of golf, the journalistic entourage has departed and I'm left with my new caddy, whose name is Khatanbaatar. With everything else going so well, the only question remaining is whether or not I'll get along with this guy. As with Sogoo, I had the same reservations about whether or not Khatan-baatar was cut out for this unique assignment. As we set up camp on the leeward side of a small knoll, I strike up a conversation to get to know him a little better.

Khatanbaatar is a fifty-seven-year-old father of six and has been a professional truck driver for many years. He has driven trucks into Russia, China, and Kazakhstan, and speaks enough of those languages to get by. He carries the large characteristic truck-driver belly well and looks young for his age—a rarity in Mongolia. Also a grandfather, his paternal instincts were evident today as he main-tained constant visual contact with me as I golfed, and twice he drove his jeep across the grass to check on me when I was approached by locals on horseback. Of course, his attentiveness will be more accurately judged when airag season approaches, but early indications are that he'll be a reliable and amiable companion.

As I prepare dinner, a brisk, steady wind causes my tiny gas-burning cookstove to roar like a dragon mouse. Khatanbaatar finishes wiping down his jeep with a large rag and takes a seat next to me on the ground. He peers into the saucepan as I stir the macaroni and canned Chinese fish. I firmly squeeze a bottle of spicy Russian ketchup, adding a generous dollop to the mix. This dish is representative of the simple cuisine that we can expect to eat for the next two months. We've got one saucepan, and our choice of ingredients was limited to what was available in the small Mongolian supermarkets.

I dump half of it into Khatanbaatar's metal tin that he uses for both food and drink. He takes a bite and pauses, contemplatively, as if this is a new experience for him. "Mmm," he says, "this is good. I like American food."

I laugh at the thought of this random concoction of international ingredients that is completely new to me being called "American food." I shove a spoonful into my mouth and give Khatanbaatar a thumbs-up. Yeah, I think I'll get along with him just fine.

Quickly, name five famous golf caddies. Okay, try naming three, or even one. Unless you're an avid golf fan, this is tough to do. It's like trying to name the first mate on Christopher Columbus's journeys. Many golfers can recall the second shot that Sandy Lyle hit out of a fairway bunker on the eighteenth hole of the 1988 Masters tournament, but no one remembers who was caddying for him that day, which is a shame because, like first mates on transatlantic ships, caddies play an important role in the successful navigation of a golf course.

Most caddies are proficient golfers themselves, just short of professional grade but certainly worthy enough to hold their own in an

amateur tournament. Along with the fourteen golf clubs that professionals are allowed to use, golf bags may contain food, water, rain
gear, extra balls and tees, players' watches and car keys, lucky
charms, and an assortment of other items that add up to about forty
pounds. Caddies carry this weight on their shoulders for eighteen
holes while providing advice on distance, weather conditions, and
club selection. It's an essential job, but a thankless one. Once a tournament begins, caddies live only to serve their employers and
receive none of the fame and glory that winning players obtain. In
exchange for this, caddies can receive either a percentage of a
player's earnings or a set salary. It's enough to make a living, but
very few caddies get rich at their job. None of them will tell you he's
in it for the money.

Khatanbaatar, on the other hand, probably *is* in it for the money,
rather than the pleasure of spending two months traveling with me
across the country. But like the caddies on the PGA tour, he also
carries about forty pounds of food, water, and gear for me, albeit in
his UAZ 469 jeep. He's also shown tremendous loyalty and self-
sacrifice in his service.

On an icy cold day on hole eleven, I was suffering with every
shot as the cold steel of the three-iron vibrated in my bare frozen
hands upon contact with the ball, sending reverberations of pain
through the tiny bones of my fingers. Since I don't normally wear a
golf glove, the idea of bringing anything to wear on my hands never
crossed my mind as I prepared for this year's expedition, a brainless

oversight that has cost me dearly. Aside from the realization of my stupidity for forgetting that even in early June the weather can be bitterly frigid, the physical pain was becoming unbearable, and I had to stop before each shot to blow several warm breaths onto my numb hands. As I walked along a steep, open hillside where the wind blew furiously, Khatanbaatar pulled up next to me, opened his door, and waved his pair of leather gloves. I wanted to kiss him.

But now on hole twelve, continuing west from Bayankhongor to Altai, I've got a few issues with him. I've begun to notice an abundance of lizards scurrying to escape my footsteps as I walk across the landscape. I've also noticed many more camels grazing in the scrubby grasslands than I've seen anywhere else in Mongolia. And as I pluck my golf ball from a cactus patch and place it on an adjacent area of loose sand, I begin to wonder if I haven't drifted too far south toward the Gobi Desert. The weather is much hotter and the terrain is looking less like a fairway and more like a sand trap. I'm no expert on Mongolian geography, but something just doesn't feel right.

At the end of the day, I plot the GPS coordinates on my map and show it to Khatanbaatar. The tiny "X" that I've just drawn in pencil is clearly and unequivocally nowhere near the road that we're supposed to be following. I wait for Khatanbaatar's reaction.

He pauses dramatically and scratches his chin before replying. "Yes," he says, "we're following a different road."

No shit! I can clearly see that we're following a different road, but the question is *Why* are we following a different road?"

"The other road crosses some mountains, but this one is much flatter," he states confidently.

This answer smells funny but he stops just short of calling it a "shortcut," so I can't be sure if he's bullshitting me or not. It's not hard to imagine that he had no idea which road we were supposed to take. That happens with regularity in Mongolia. Even experienced drivers get lost all the time. The dirt tracks across the vast expanses of this country sometimes split up, veer off, or multiply into a myriad of possible paths, creating a navigational nightmare. There are no road signs, and it's possible to travel for hours without seeing any inhabitants who might be able give some directional advice.

In my current situation, it doesn't seem like I have much of a choice. I've made the decision long ago to trust Khatanbaatar with choosing the right path. Every day, he drives his jeep ahead of me and I hit the ball in his direction. It's a role that he has enthusiastically adopted, and to change it now would jeopardize our relationship. Pondering my limited options, I'm reminded of a story that a British expatriate living in Ulaan Baatar told last year.

She was riding in the back seat of a taxi and attempted to tell the driver to make a left turn. "*Zuun,*" she said, using the Mongolian word for "left." But the driver continued driving straight ahead, or *chigeeree* in Mongolian. She summed up the story with one phrase: "I said zuun, fate said chigeeree."

The story, and that last phrase in particular, struck a chord with all the foreigners living in Mongolia. As a stranger in a strange land, you have to accept that you don't have complete control over—or even a complete understanding of—the events that happen to you or happen around you. The barriers can be cultural, lingual, or legal, and they take a lot of time and effort to overcome. The most effective survival strategy in these circumstances is to remain calm and accept that sometimes fate takes you in a new direction.

"Do you want to go back to the other road?" Khatanbaatar asks me.

I lift my gaze up from the map (which doesn't clearly show any significant mountains in the path of the other road) and stare toward the setting sun and the road ahead. With a snap of my wrist, I point in this direction and answer Khatanbaatar with one word. "Chigeeree!"

But this detour isn't the only imperfection I've noticed in Khatanbaatar. There's another common problem with many Mongolians that I've begun to notice. This problem has to do with distance measurement.

Until the time when science could measure the speed of light in a vacuum tube, there existed in Paris a titanium rod that measured exactly one meter. This rod was meant to define a standard, consistent unit of distance that was to be accepted the world over. In a time when science and world trade were still evolving, this consistency was needed. It was globalism in its infant stages. But even now, in the twenty-first century, there's still a need for that same consistency—in Mongolia. In fact, there are many days when I wish I had a titanium rod to hand out to every man, woman, and child in the country.

In planning where the two of us eat and sleep each night, it's useful to know the locations of tiny villages or roadside gers that serve hot meals. I can vary the distance I golf in a day by a few kilometers if there's a logical reason to do so. I commonly ask Khatanbaatar, or any locals who I happen to meet, "How far is it to the next village?" The answers invariably come back with an implied measure of exactitude such as "seventeen kilometers." In my mind, when someone says seventeen kilometers, they're pretty sure it's not sixteen or eighteen, and there's no way that it's twenty-five. Yet these gross misestimations of distance occur here, and they seem to do so with unsettling regularity. Despite the fact that the locals give such precise answers, the real distance generally varies from their estimate by 20 to 30 percent. I shouldn't let this bother me. I'm an explorer, for God's sake. I thrive on the unexpected and unpredictable. But I was trained as an engineer with a great respect for precision, and my favorite pastime is a sport where accurately knowing distances is critical. I imagine that if Tiger Woods asked his caddy, Steve Williams, how many yards it was to the hole and the answer came back "157 yards," he'd assume it to be quite accurate. One hundred fifty-six or 158 would be within the realm of possibility, but anything outside this deviation would be unacceptable. Should the distance be 167 yards, perchance, well then old

Steve-o would quickly find himself back in New Zealand contemplating the exact dimensions of his sheep paddock.

These errors have caused me to golf for long stretches on an empty stomach or with my water bottle desperately in need of a refill. Just yesterday, I told Khatanbaatar that we should meet in three kilometers to have lunch, thinking that I could put off my hunger for about an hour. Two hours and six kilometers later, I finally reached his jeep, agitated by an empty stomach and low energy level. But I refrain from bitching about it, because it's this same mentality in the Mongolian people that produces seemingly precise, yet horribly misconceived, estimates of distance that I admire most about them. They can do anything they need to do in order to get by in life, and this seems to lead them to believe that they can do everything well. It's not arrogance, it's self-confidence, and self-confidence in the most innocent way. I've tried to correct their perceptions of distance at times by showing them my GPS unit and the precision to which it can measure the distance between two points, but I think they've always been skeptical, staring at my hand-held device the way that the Arawak and Taino people probably reacted when Christopher Columbus calmly and assuredly informed them that they were living near the sub-continent of India.

These encounters raise the question of the value of technology. If the entire village believes that it's seventeen kilometers to the next village, then so be it, it's seventeen kilometers. What difference does it really make if they're wrong? What use would a

Global Positioning System have for a nomadic herder? Absolutely none at all.

The contrast between vagueness and exactitude that I've noticed in the calculation of distance here can be observed as a more general phenomenon of the culture. In an agrarian society, activities are more related to the weather or the changing of the seasons than to a clock or calendar. No one cares if they've worked eight hours or twelve hours in a day, as long as they've completed the day's work. The Lonely Planet guidebook calls Mongolia "a land without fences"; and in the countryside, this is still true. As long as there's plenty of pasture in which one's animals can graze, there's no need to fence any of it off, or to even measure it in acres. Mongolians know how to survive in this land, but they'd surely never survive a day as caddies on the PGA tour.

As I proceed west over the next three days, the desert scenery proceeds with me. This unexpected encounter with a new land-scape has presented three unique challenges. First, finding a playable lie has become increasingly difficult. Over the course of more than eight thousand shots, I've learned a lot about the various species of vegetation on the Mongolian steppe. While a botanist might be able to say that I've moved from a zone where *Stipa baicalensis* and *Cleistogenes sqarrosa* are common to an area where *Stipa gobica* and *Cleistogenes soongorica* are more prevalent, all I can say is that the golf conditions are crap here. There's a definite scarcity of *Grassus golfus*.

If you've ever gone for a walk on a beach, then you can empathize with me about my second problem. Walking on loose sand is fatiguing. Hitting 150 shots and covering more than twenty-five kilometers each day already push me close to my physical limit. Trying to continue this rate of progress on unconsolidated sand is impossible. I constantly survey the landscape ahead and often make wide detours to avoid these areas of loose sand, like a sailor avoiding uncharted reefs and shoals.

Third, it's an inferno here. The Mongolian summer has made a dramatic and rapid entrance. Where just a week ago I was freezing my digits off, now I'm roasting like a marmot on a spit. The barren sandy terrain that I pass over soaks up the sun's energy and radiates it back at me from below like a double broiler. I begin to wonder if the allegedly "mountainous" road might have offered some cool "mountain" breezes.

But just as every cactus contains a moist heart and every treacherous golf course has a nineteenth hole, every desert must have an oasis. On June 11, I find it. High in the Khangai mountain range, two hundred kilometers to the north, a winter's worth of snowfall slowly melts to form a lifeline of pure, frigid bliss that extends itself down into the Gobi Desert like spilled coins from Donald Trump's pockets. The Baidrag River is only a knee-deep slice of refreshment across this arid region; but in these parts, where the moisture-impoverished voices from parched mouths and dusty throats beg for relief, even trickle-down economics is better than none at all.

Desert oases are special places. Like a safe harbor in a tempes-
tuous sea, an oasis offers a refuge from the elements. An opportunity to forget the harshness of nature's fury and revel instead in one
of her joyous creations. This tiny river is not a literal oasis in the
geographical sense, but the effect that it has on passing travelers or
overheated animals is the same.

Young girls squeal as boys toss bucketfuls of ice-cold water on
them. Horses stand immobile in the middle of the stream with the
rushing water flowing briskly past their ankles. And one lone
golfer strips down to his underclothes, revealing the stunning pig-
mental contrast of his "golfer's tan," and lies flat on the rocky river
bottom, completely submerged in the water. The latter happens
upstream of the horses, I might add.

Khatanbaatar kneels over a green plastic basin on the pebble-
strewn shore and vigorously rubs a bar of soap across his shirt,
which he alternately dunks and wrings in the basin. I lift my head
above the water surface and return from the underwater dream-
world into which I had escaped. Khatanbaatar looks over at me and
laughs. "André! Hee hee, it's good isn't it? Hee hee hee."

Even this fifty-seven-year-old grandfather is seduced into
behaving like a young boy by the magical qualities of this river. I
give him a silent thumbs-up sign and resubmerge my head under
the water. My outstretched arms hold onto two stones and my body
becomes suspended in the river's current, hidden from the world.
Like a child's blanket, the cool water currents billow around my

body, providing a safe haven from the harshness of the external environment. The gurgling flux of the water and its swirling eddies are all I hear in this insulated cosmos of security. With my eyes closed, I fly through the water, far upstream to a land of snow and ice. I dart and turn at supersonic speed through all the oceans of the world. I visit paradises of calmness, edens of tranquility, and rapturous utopias all in a matter of seconds. For a brief moment, I escape from the confinement of my body. It's an escape that I desperately needed.

Like buyer's remorse two weeks after the purchase of a new car, the initial excitement of resuming my golf adventure has worn off. There are hundreds of kilometers of Mongolian countryside still ahead of me, and I have to hit this little white ball across them all. The physical ailments that I experienced last year have made their return—sore feet, blisters on the hands, and general fatigue. These nagging problems have been recently joined by a more serious malady, an increasingly painful left knee. The words "anterior cruciate ligament" come to mind, but there are no doctors to visit in this part of the world, and certainly no arthroscopic surgeons to provide a qualified medical opinion. The decision I make regarding this ailment would exasperate any qualified medical professional: I ignore this obvious signal from my body that something is wrong, and hope that the pain will go away.

Along with a stubborn determination, it is hope and optimism that have brought me this far. "Things will get better," I've told myself over and over since I left Choibalsan and began play on the first of eighteen of the longest golf holes in the world. Twelve holes are now complete. Hope, like that of a nameless sailor on a fifteenth-century caravel somewhere in the Atlantic, has not failed me yet. As I rise and stand again on solid ground, leaving the Baidrag River's transformative influence behind, hope will be an important crutch for my ailing knee and my peace of mind.

Despite all the magical qualities of revival that the Baidrag River provides to me and all the other passersby who have frolicked in its waters, a cold, harsh fact remains: the Baidrag River flows into the Gobi Desert and dies. Its rapid but joyful life terminates suddenly and completely in the overpowering vacuousness of the desert, never to be heard from again. My fate, I can only hope, will be significantly better than this.

It's hard to say what influence the caddy, Dave Musgrove, had on the most important shot of Sandy Lyle's career in 1988, just as it's difficult to say if Columbus would have ever found the West Indies without the services of competent first mates on his three ships. But I know for sure that without a caddy, I never would have made it this far. And after my restorative visit to this river oasis, I'm happy to have Khatanbaatar provide the necessary guidance for the long road ahead, no matter how many kilometers it is.

lthough there are eighteen golf holes across Mongolia, only six of them share a special significance. These are the six that end in the capitals of Mongolian provinces. These cities generally have populations of fifteen to twenty-five thousand and serve as the political and economic centers of their provinces. Where life in the countryside hasn't significantly changed in thousands of years, these cities, for the most part, contain the only evidence that modern technology has reached Mongolia at all. Along with their significance to the locals as public transportation hubs and regional markets, these six waypoints on my journey serve several important functions in terms of my expedition's success.

First, I can stock up on food provisions at the open markets or small grocery stores. Second, I can access a rudimentary but mostly functioning telephone system. Third, I can access the Internet and communicate with family and friends though e-mail, albeit over a painfully slow connection. Fourth, I can take a night off from my tent and sleep in a real bed in one of the city's rapidly deteriorating hotels. And finally, I can take a hot shower at the city's public bathhouse.

The shower, as you might guess, is at the top of the priority list as I arrive in the city of Altai, the capital of Gov-Altai Province. A small concrete building sits on an empty lot of dirt and broken concrete in a neighborhood of mixed residential and commercial use. The only indication that this is a bath house is the tall smokestack that rises from the back of the building, supported by guywires and attached to a coal- or wood-fired boiler. I pay the entrance fee of eight hundred tögrög (seventy-five cents) and, after a ten-minute wait, one of the shower stalls becomes vacant and I'm led inside by an old Mongolian woman who gives me a pair of plastic sandals. It's the kind of place where I can imagine a yuppie urbanite standing in the doorway saying "You expect me to take a shower . . . *in there?*" The paint is peeling from the mildew-stained walls, and the floor is partially covered by a waterlogged wooden pallet. Its uninviting character doesn't deter me in the slightest, however, because I know from the amount of steam in the air that the water is going to be piping hot, a luxury that I've sorely missed.

Standing under the dribble of a rusty shower head, I watch as the water flows from my body and coalesces into a dark brown stream the color of the Mississippi Delta, and then runs toward a floor drain. Two weeks of dust, caked in layers of daily sweat, is coming off my skin. It takes three renditions of "lather, rinse, and repeat" to get my grungy hair clean again. Aside from my splash in the Baidrag River, this is the first opportunity I've had to bathe since departing the city of Bayankhongor sixteen days ago. It's also the last opportunity I'll have for a hot shower until I reach Khovd, the finishing point for the expedition.

I spend my full quota of thirty minutes in the shower scrubbing myself, washing a shirt and a pair of underwear (the ones that I'll wear for the next three weeks), and hacking away at a substantial growth of facial hair with a disposable razor. When I finally emerge from the shower stall and step into the lobby where some young women are working, I feel like a new man, which is fitting because today also happens to be my birthday. The women giggle and tell me how handsome I look and that they almost didn't recognize me. Apparently these waters have magical qualities as well.

The city of Altai sits at an elevation of 2,181 meters, or 7,156 feet. The high altitude has provided some pleasantly cool weather and, more importantly, some excellent golfing conditions. My brief run-in with the Gobi ended just a few days after I hit the ball across the Baidrag River, and the terrain quickly regained its fairwaylike qualities. In fact, the thirteenth and fourteenth holes provided some of the best golfing conditions that I have experienced anywhere in Mongolia. Khatanbaatar's choice of roads, as it turns out, worked out beautifully. His navigational abilities now indisputably established, he rose even higher on the caddy charts when, after a celebratory birthday dinner complete with canned Korean beer, he presented me with a box of chocolates as a gift.

The following day, we depart the city and I begin the fifteenth hole of golf near Altai's airport. If I had wanted to, I could have golfed right down the middle of the runway. Post-9/11 security measures haven't reached this tiny landing strip where the weekly arrivals and departures can be jotted on the back of a ten-tögrög note. Grazing horses and cows are more of a concern to pilots than potential hijackers.

Soon, I reach the highest point of my journey at 2,300 meters (7,546 feet) above sea level and begin my descent through a steep canyon. This is the Khan Taishiriin mountain range; and, over the next several days, I steadily drop down into the belly of the beast. I call it that because in Mongolian, this region is known as the *khuisiin govi,* or belly button desert. There are dozens of named desert regions in Mongolia, and this one has the pleasure of being named after a detritus-collecting navel. It's a fitting name, not only because the contours on my local map form concentric rings in an oblong navel-shaped pattern, but also because of the scattered boulders, prickly shrubs, and dry riverbeds that give it the appearance of a refuse-laden wasteland. Stagnant pools of brackish water surrounded by bleached-white salt flats and tall reeds dot the region. But its hellish qualities don't end there.

It is interminably hot. It's as if the cool winds have forsaken this area and left it to stew in its own warm air like the inside of a goat's belly. Amidst this sweltering inferno, another incomprehensibly unlikely annoyance has presented itself—mosquitoes. I've suffered the wrath of swarming mosquitoes in the Siberian taiga and the wetlands of South America. In those places, the presence of blood-sucking insects is understandable. But mosquitoes in a desert? What sick bastard came up with that idea?

Several days of swatting insects while trying to swat golf balls follow until, one afternoon, we reach a collection of a dozen gers strewn along a section of the road. The gers are tucked into a barren valley with bright ochre-red rock outcroppings sprouting out of the landscape, but there is little vegetation. Tufts of tall grass are randomly scattered about, and the lack of rain has left last year's dry brown vegetation as the dominant ground cover. One lone well sits in a low sandy depression in the middle of the gers. The well provides life-giving water not only for the families living here, but also for their animals, and for Khatanbaatar and me who replenish our two plastic jugs with several plunges of the hand pump.

Khatanbaatar had preceded me to this little hamlet and parked next to one of the gers. His green jeep was easily recognizable, as it was one of two vehicles in the village; and after I hit my final shot of the day, I walked in that direction. Khatanbaatar emerged from the ger with a crowd of people who had anticipated my imminent arrival and wanted to be among the first to see the lone foreigner walking across their country hitting a golf ball. Like many of my encounters with small villages, the atmosphere surrounding my arrival is part visiting dignitary and part circus.

As I glance at Khatanbaatar, I notice something different about him. He's wearing polished black leather shoes and a clean button-down shirt, and his thinning hair is combed nicely back. It turns out that the people around him are his in-laws. Exactly how the relations work I can't quite understand, and perhaps even Khatanbaatar doesn't know precisely who's who, for he'd never met them before. But I do figure out that his wife's father is a well-known figure from this region of the country. It's not unusual for a Mongolian person to have never met his or her extended family. It's an enormous country, and people in the rural areas don't frequently travel. Geneticists have said that one out of every two hundred men on earth has some relationship to Genghis Khan, and obviously this proportion is higher among Mongolians. Using this knowledge, one could assume that most Mongolians are related in some way and that the exact branching of family trees is less important than the culture of hospitality, which is offered to all strangers. A culture reinforced, no doubt, by the fact that you never know which stranger might just be your second cousin, once removed.

Mongolian family trees took a serious blow in the 1920s, when the new communist government eliminated all family names by government order. After that time, all Mongolians would be known only by their father's name (often abbreviated as a single letter) and one given name. Thus, if Damdinsuren had a daughter named Altantsetseg, she would officially be recognized as D. Altantsetseg. This system dismantled any claims to descent from Mongolia's noble clans, an effective means of establishing equality among the citizenry in line with communist principles, and of preventing any clan-based challenge to the new government's authority. But as the knowledge of family lineage became lost, diversity of genetic stock could not be assured and problems with inbreeding grew. Recent governments have tried to resolve this problem with the reintroduction of family names, but genetic diversity is still a problem.

I've visited dozens of random families all across the country, and I've observed numerous individuals who appear to be mentally retarded. Whether this is due to iodine deficiency or inbreeding is difficult to tell. But with such a low population density in the countryside and no family names as guides, it's easy to believe that genetics is somehow involved.

I'm not sure if it's a genetic problem or not, but one of Khatanbaatar's relatives has a serious saliva problem. More accurately, anyone who talks to him has a serious saliva problem. I have no idea what his real name is, but I've taken to calling him Spitting Sam.

Spitting Sam isn't a close-talker or a loud-talker; he's a spit-talker. As soon as I met him, I had the urge to shout a phrase I haven't used since elementary school: "Say it, don't spray it!" Granted, he appears to have already gotten to know the contents of a vodka bottle or two, but I've never met anyone so salivatorily challenged before. The ejaculated particles of spit that emanate from his mouth as he talks create a moisture assault of epic proportions. He might single-handedly be able to solve all of Mongolia's drought problems. I constantly try to back away from him as he talks, but he's a big man with enormous hands and he has the habit of firmly gripping my forearm as he spit-talks to me. I use the back of my hand to wipe the spit from my face, but this doesn't get the message through. To make matters worse, he's instantly taken a liking to me and seems determined to engage me in a splatter-filled conversation. As we enter the ger, I fear that he'll take a seat next to me and continue the assault, but fortunately there is a distraction.

Propped on the top of a suitcase, which in turn sits atop a cardboard box, is a small black-and-white television. A large group of children sits on the floor around the TV, mesmerized by a cartoon. Even the adults fix their gaze on the set in between bits of conversation and the consumption of milk tea and snacks. The TV is run by electricity from a solar panel. I've seen dozens of solar panels as I've moved across the country this year, compared to only a few last year, and none at all when I visited in 2001; a sure sign that the times are quickly changing. The apparatus is the size of a small card table and is mounted on a short pole which can be rotated manually to follow the sun. The units cost about $200—a lot of money for a rural family—but apparently Khatanbaatar's relatives see it as a worthwhile investment, as it gives them enough power to run a couple of lightbulbs and their television and satellite dish. The sight of a large parabolic satellite dish sitting next to a felt-and-canvas home in the middle of the Mongolia steppe is full of contradictions but indicative of the rapid changes to rural life in Mongolia.

For better *and* for worse, technology has dramatically altered life for many of the world's poor or remote people. Television just recently reached the country of Bhutan, for example, and anthropologists say that it has caused the indigenous culture irreparable damage. But anthropologists don't run the world, and if the Bhutanese want television, then who's to condemn it?

As evening slowly arrives, the TV stays on and the cartoons give way to a Mongolian romantic comedy series, followed by the 1934 Frank Capra classic *It Happened One Night,* starring Clark Gable, whose voice is dubbed simultaneously into Russian and Mongolian (the Mongolian slightly louder), and then the second half of a Euro Cup soccer match between France and Greece. Not an avid television viewer normally, I even find myself enthralled by the little box with moving pictures in this setting, especially when Greece scores a brilliant goal to seal the victory against the French.

It's odd to think that tourists come to Mongolia precisely because the country offers an escape from technology and the demands it puts on their lives, yet Mongolians want to increase its role in their own lives. Even during my first visit to the country, I found it "charming" that there were no TVs in most rural homes. Now here I am after a month without TV, and I can't take my eyes off it. It's a startling realization that the appeal of modern technology is virtually unstoppable. Once the existence of a new technology becomes known, human nature will create a desire for it.

When I arrived in Altai, one of my first tasks was accessing the Internet and checking my e-mail. I've only regularly used e-mail for about five years, yet I can't imagine life without it. As Mongolia strives to improve the quality of life of its citizens, technology will play an increasingly important role, and life as most Mongolians know it will change dramatically. How these changes will affect Mongolian society is unknown. I'm not even sure how my own life will change in the near future. But for now, I'm happy to sit quietly and wait for the next movie to start. Especially if it keeps the spit-filled conversation to a minimum.

Two men pull up to the ger on a 125cc Russian-made Planeta motorcycle and come inside. One has a ballot box in his hands, and the other carries a notebook and a stack of ballots. It's June 27, election day in Mongolia, and, in the countryside, the ballot box makes house calls. I'm tempted to imagine that this system could introduce corruption into the electoral process, but when I see Khatanbaatar, the men on the motorcycle, and one of the neighbors open a bottle of vodka after the votes have been cast, I feel more reassured. As previously noted, vodka is a serious drink to be enjoyed on serious occasions, and it's hard for me to imagine that foul play could be involved in any way with this ritual.

I pass on the vodka. It's 10:00 A.M., and I still have twenty-five kilometers to golf today. But I'm extremely curious as to how this voting process works. Khatanbaatar and I have spent the night in the ger of his in-laws, and we had just finished a bowl of soup when the election officials arrived. Khatanbaatar is far from his home in Ulaan Baatar, but he has apparently filled out the proper paperwork that allows him to cast a ballot. We've chatted about politics over the past few weeks, and he's made it very clear that in these Parliamentary elections that are now taking place, he supports the Mongolian People's Revolutionary Party (the MPRP). All seventy-six seats in Mongolia's parliament (the Great Khural) are up for grabs today, and the winning party will choose the prime minister and cabinet members. My golfing expedition aside, this is by far the biggest event on Mongolia's 2004 calendar.

Mongolia has a pragmatic political history that's been shaped by necessity. Located between two enormous powers, China and Russia, the survival of the land as an autonomous nation-state has always depended upon its leaders' savvy and deftness in playing one side against the other. In the early twentieth century, the Qing dynasty collapsed in China, the Bolshevik revolution took place in Russia, and Japan began to expand its sphere of influence in Asia. The future was uncertain for Mongolia, which had previously been governed by China, and an alliance with Soviet Russia was chosen as the most certain way to ensure some degree of independence. This alliance was strengthened in 1921 when Mongolia became the

I GOLFED ACROSS MONGOLIA

world's second Communist country, and the Communist MPRP
was born.

The MPRP governed Mongolia unopposed for the next seventy
years. Some historians would say that Mongolia was essentially a
puppet state of the Soviet Union during this time and that it took
all its orders from its Communist brothers in Moscow. Evidence of
this is clear in the Stalinist-style purges of the 1930s and in
Moscow's support for Mongolian politicians who toed the line of
Soviet political philosophy. This relationship brought security to
Mongolia's autonomy and also allowed a scientific and educational
exchange to develop not only with the Soviet Union but also with
Poland, East Germany, and other Eastern European nations. Most
of the industrialization and infrastructure of Mongolia was
financed with Soviet funds, and, because of this, Russians are still
seen in a positive light, especially in contrast to the public percep-
tion of the Chinese, whom the Mongolians distrust.

The influence of the Soviet Union in Eastern Europe and Central Asia began to crumble in 1989 and 1990, as the citizens of these
countries revolted and demanded an end to their one-party political
systems. The Berlin Wall was thousands of miles from Mongolia,
but its collapse had a significant impact on the country's history. In
1990, demonstrations and hunger strikes began to take place in
Ulaan Baatar, as democracy advocates put demands on the MPRP
to hold free and fair democratic elections. In stark contrast to the
events of Tiananmen Square which had occurred just a year earlier

in Beijing, the MPRP submitted peacefully and agreed to new elections. Mongolians would get their first chance to choose a new government.

Despite the protests, hunger strikes, and demonstrations against the ruling government that prompted the elections, the MPRP won. Compared to other nations where dramatic revolutions produced completely new governments, this was astonishing, and it's even more surprising that the world hardly noticed. This was perhaps the only country where a one-party Communist state held free elections and the existing government remained in control. The Mongolian people exercised their new rights, and as a testament to their conservative and practical dispositions, they saw no better alternative than to re-elect those leaders in the existing government. Political opponents of the MPRP claimed that this was because the opposition didn't have enough time to organize themselves; but when elections were held next, in 1992, the MPRP won again.

Communism as Mongolia knew it was abandoned, however, as the reshaped MPRP began the privatization process and opened the country to foreign investors. This was a necessary step, since the 30 percent of Mongolia's economy that had come from direct aid from the Soviet Union had disappeared. Still pragmatic in their political philosophy, Mongolia began new trade relationships with Japan, Korea, Europe, and the United States. In fact, much of the thirty percent of the economy that was lost from the Soviet Union was replaced with foreign aid from new international donors. The

MPRP had held control unopposed for seventy years and had just won two consecutive democratic elections. They weren't going to give up power easily.

Change finally arrived in 1996, when the Democratic Party won the parliamentary elections, putting an end to seventy-five years of continuous MPRP governance. Amid corruption scandals and mismanagement, the Democratic Party went through several prime ministers in their first years in control. They did such a poor job of running the country that when the elections of 2000 rolled around, the MPRP won back 72 of 76 seats in the parliament. The MPRP itself was not free from scandal or allegations of corruption either. A free press emerged in the 1990s that, with varying degrees of journalistic integrity, took relentless aim at the country's politicians and exposed several major scandals. The growing pains of a new democracy with new freedoms of speech and expression were becoming evident, and the Mongolian people were increasingly distrustful of politicians and cynical about the political process. Political surveys of the last few years show that a majority of people believe that the MPRP is more corrupt than the Democratic Party, but that they trust the MPRP to take care of their interests more. Given Mongolians' pragmatic attitudes toward politics, somehow this makes sense. And now, the elections of 2004 had arrived.

The MPRP mounted a full-fledged campaign to remain in control. They plastered Ulaan Baatar with billboards, aired advertisements on the state-run television station, and canvassed the countryside in a grassroots effort to gain the people's favor, distributing posters and calendars displaying the party logo. They even constructed a giant MPRP sign (MAXH in Cyrillic), made of painted stones, on the hillside across the Tuul River that was dominatingly visible from downtown Ulaan Baatar. The prevailing opinion among political experts was that they were going to win this election fairly easily. Even some supporting the Democratic Party silently expressed their hope to take just 20 out of the 76 parliament seats. The MPRP only needed to win 39 out of its 72 current seats to maintain majority control.

While optimism was held to a minimum among the Democratic Party members, they certainly weren't giving up without a fight. They'd forged alliances with several other smaller parties to form a stronger coalition, the Motherland Democracy Coalition (MDC).

Mongolians tend to be tight-lipped when discussing politics. Perhaps this is due to a history of political repression. For seventy years, the MPRP instituted a policy where dissenters of the party's view were ostracized—or, worse, purged. But I do get Khatanbaatar to share his views with me. He's outspoken in his support of the MPRP. I don't know how to say MPRP in Mongolian, so I refer to them by their party slogan, which I've seen often in the previous weeks: *"Tany Tölöö, Tantai Khamt."* I loosely, and maybe incorrectly, translate this as "on your behalf, together with you" Khatanbaatar also favors the war in Iraq and thinks George W. Bush is a good man. He isn't alone in this opinion, as Mongolia has sent several hundred troops to Iraq to join America's Operation Iraqi Freedom. One Mongolian soldier became a national hero when he shot the driver of a truck laden with explosives before it reached the gates of a Coalition military base housing 9,500 multi-national soldiers in Hilla, just south of Baghdad. Khatanbaatar points to his forehead as he proudly describes the events that were replayed on the Mongolian news: "One bullet, through the windshield, right between the eyes."

Mongolia joining the "coalition of the willing" by sending a military presence to Iraq does represent a developing foreign policy. There are military attachés from three countries that are permanently stationed in Mongolia: its two neighbors, China and Russia, and the United States. The old Russian military bases in Mongolia are abandoned and deteriorating, while the United States is taking part in joint training exercises with Mongolian troops across the country. Without reading too much into it, it's easy to speculate where Mongolia's national security policy is headed in the context of Northeast Asian regional security issues. But the question of who would steer this policy is yet to be determined. First, a parliament has to be elected, and a prime minister chosen.

That choice is now taking place in individual gers scattered across the countryside, like the one I'm sitting in right now. I'm amused by the vodka-drinking election officials and the mobile ballot box, and I get Khatanbaatar to pose for a photo as he drops his ballot into the light blue plastic box. This is real democracy in action, and the

Mongolian people have taken their responsibility seriously. In this year's parliamentary elections, 80 percent of eligible voters will cast ballots, compared to 40 percent in the last congressional elections in the United States and 45 percent in the 2004 European Union parliamentary elections. Perhaps our Western countries could use some vodka and socializing to increase the participation rates.

But the casting of the ballots is only the first step of the elections. The *counting* of the ballots is equally important; and, as this process takes place, the country is thrown into turmoil and faces the most serious test of its fourteen-year democratic history.

Compared to the election coverage in the United States, where every TV station broadcasts results and endless analysis in real time as news emerges from various polling stations, definitive election results in Mongolia are frustratingly slow in coming. News travels slowly and mostly by word of mouth in the countryside; and, compounding this, my Mongolian language skills aren't strong enough to even understand the names of the parties, let alone the nuances of political jargon. I get a clearer picture of the election developments three days later, as Khatanbaatar and I sit in a ger while a woman and her young daughter make homemade mutton dumplings for our lunch. A small transistor radio hangs from one of the eighty-one support poles that bear the weight of the ger's conical canvas roof. The station interrupts its program of classical Mongolian music to bring news from the capital city. I watch Khatanbaatar to gauge his reaction.

He drops his chin down and shakes his head, then begins an animated discussion with the woman in the ger. It looks like bad news for the MPRP; but I want to be sure, so I clear my throat and interrupt.

"Tany tölöö, tantai khamt, how many?" I ask, referring to the MPRP by their slogan.

Khatanbaatar is amused by my interest. "Thirty-six," he replies.

"Gundalai, how many?" I follow up, referring to the MDC by the Democratic Party's most outspoken Member of Parliament, Mr. Gundalai. (I haven't yet learned how to say Motherland Democratic Coalition.)

"Thirty-six," he answers with an air of disgust.

I later learn that four independent candidates also won, to round out the seventy-six seats. Incredibly, the elections have ended in a tie. But the results are not as clear-cut as they suggest. With the balance of power very much in limbo, both parties scramble to use whatever mechanisms they can to achieve a controlling majority. Political chaos soon erupts in the capital.

At one point, the MDC storms the MPRP-run national television station and takes it over for a couple hours, hoping to get an upper hand in the propaganda battle. Realizing that this strategy could backfire and cause more harm than good to their reputation, they finally turn the building back over to the MPRP-influenced station managers. In a situation that is eerily reminiscent of the Florida election fiasco in the year 2000, both parties begin to demand recounts of the results, and to use the judicial process to stop recounts where they imagine them to be unfavorable. Mongolia faces its first serious constitutional crisis.

I get daily updates from Khatanbaatar, who monitors the situation by chatting with every truck driver he sees along the lonely roads of western Mongolia. One day the MPRP looks to have the upper hand, and the next day the MDC appears to gain control as results in several districts change after recounts or, in some cases, completely new revotes. But as the political and constitutional battles continue, momentum never swings strongly in either direction and stalemate seems inevitable. The independent candidates have aligned themselves in a way that doesn't shift the balance of power to one side of the aisle or the other. Finally, a compromise is reached.

The MDC will choose the prime minister, the MPRP will select the Speaker of the Parliament, and cabinet positions will be split between the two parties. It will be a true bipartisan coalition government.

It's astounding that a country with only a fourteen-year history of multiparty democracy could find such an elegant solution to the crisis. Contrasting this to the 2000 presidential election in the United States, it seems especially sophisticated. It would be impossible to imagine, for instance, that George W. Bush and Al Gore would agree that one of them would be president for two years and the other for two years. Two hundred years of democracy in the

United States have not advanced the political process to better represent the desires of its citizens. In fact, politicians seem more polarized than ever, and common-sense compromises that most citizens would favor are unlikely to occur because of this polarization. In this small Central Asian nation of two and a half million people, the inherent belief of pragmatic political philosophy has ruled the day. Although Mongolians are passionate about their political beliefs and party loyalties, almost all of them agree that the recent compromise is a good thing.

A week after election day, politics is still the topic on everyone's mind, and I find myself an observer of a political debate in one of the most unusual places I've ever spent a night. After twenty-four kilometers of golf, Khatanbaatar and I were setting up camp on a rocky dirt slope when a young man approached on a motorcycle. He tells us that he works nights in a cellular phone signal tower on the top of a nearby hill, and that we should come and spend the night up there. We don't hesitate to accept his invitation and soon follow him up a winding dirt road that leads to an octagonal building built around an enormous ten-foot-diameter steel tower that holds several antennas. Inside, the tower is covered in electrical panel boards with dials, switches, and meters protruding out into the narrow control room. A small doorway leads to the only other room, which houses a generator and other equipment. Along with the inner workings of the station, the main control room also features a metal bedframe with a thin mattress, an electric hotplate-style cooking burner, a small table, and two chairs. Khatanbaatar and I are offered the chairs as the man tells us that his wife will be coming up later to cook dinner. I've been entertained in dozens of Mongolian gers all across the country, and during my world travels of the past three years I've slept in some odd places, but this has got to be the most bizarre.

The young man takes two wires from the back of a small television and jury-rigs them into one of the electrical panels. He smiles as he switches on the TV, proud of the accoutrements of his little home-away-from-home where he works twelve hours every day. Unable to understand much, I drift in and out of the conversation as Khatanbaatar and the man chat until a news report about the elections comes on the TV and they become silent. I can hear from the numbers that it still appears to be deadlocked between the two parties and neither Khatanbaatar nor our host seems very excited about it. But for very different reasons. The tower maintenance worker supports the Democratic Party and begins debating the merits of the party with Khatanbaatar. They engage in a friendly joust of political opinion until the maintenance worker turns to me and asks what I think of the two parties.

Most expatriates living in Mongolia favor the Democratic Party as the least corrupt and most progressive political force in the country; and from what I've heard from young Mongolians living in the capital city, I would have to agree with them. But I don't want to upset Khatanbaatar, so I wait a couple seconds before answering and stare at the television, which is now showing a Bollywood musical with a Hindi soundtrack and Mongolian subtitles.

"I think both parties are good," I finally answer.

The two men smile, knowing that my neutral answer is simply and obviously meant only to placate them both. Then Khatanbaatar says something that I've heard before from other Mongolians.

"André," he says, "what Mongolia needs is another Genghis Khan. If we're ever going to be a great nation again, then we need a great leader."

The maintenance worker nods his head. Like all Mongolians, he's a direct descendant of those warriors who swept across Central Asia, the Middle East, and Eastern Europe eight hundred years ago, conquering all the lands that lay before them, creating the largest empire in the world's history. Establishing an equally dominant geopolitical influence today will be difficult for this country. But they've chosen democracy as a means to that end, and the mobile ballot box, ceremonial vodka shots, and an engaged electorate are clear signs that Mongolians have the courage to march down that road without forgetting the greatness of their history or the atavistic strength of their culture.

The golf ball rockets off the club face toward a cloudless blue sky. A perfect white orb, reflecting the morning sun against a rich blue canvas as it spins furiously in the air and hangs for a moment before succumbing to gravity and dropping gently back to earth. It's a sight that I've witnessed more than twelve thousand times in Mongolia as I've traversed this country from east to west, and one that I've never grown tired of. The perfect golf shot brings a feeling of satisfaction that those who have never played the game are unlikely to understand. It's incredible how far a golf ball can travel when perfectly hit—defying one's intuitive assumptions of our physical world as it flies beyond the limits of our visual accuracy. Quite simply, it's a thing of beauty.

Golfers always love watching the perfect shot, but the beauty is enhanced when it takes place in an equally perfect setting such as an early-morning tee time in the middle of the week when there are no other golfers on the course, the air slightly crisp but warming steadily as the sun rises to burn the morning dew off the grass. The morning light makes the greens greener, the blues bluer, and exaggerates the brilliant white of a shining golf ball soaring through space. The perfect shot in this setting is like a lovers' kiss on a cobblestone bridge in Paris, a baseball game at Fenway Park, or a piña colada at sunset on a Caribbean beach. It just doesn't get any better.

Through the pain and fatigue, the swarming flies and mosquitoes, and the stresses of uncertainty in my long expedition, it's been these perfect shots in this country where no other golfer shares the fairway with me that have kept me going. The geography of Mongolia, while intimidating, is awesomely inspiring and has provided me with that perfect setting to clear my mind, focus on my golf swing, and attempt the perfect shot. Today, the picturesque setting of jagged snow-capped peaks in the distance and eagles hovering high overhead in an azure sky gives me yet another reason to appreciate this improbable but wonderful adventure that I've chosen. But my personal sentiments are stirred not just by the raw natural beauty that surrounds me, but by what the narrow mountain pass that cuts into a ridge of sharp black-rock hills signifies. Just over this gentle slope lies the city of Khovd—and the finish line that I've been anticipating for more than a year.

Less than a kilometer ahead of me, Khatanbaatar strolls around his parked jeep and walks toward an *ovoo*, a large pile of stones, skulls, and prayer flags that is a collection of offerings to the gods. Ovoos can be found near the top of almost any hill or mountain pass in Mongolia, and are a strong symbol of Mongolians' shamanistic beliefs. I've passed hundreds of ovoos on my trek across the country, and I've added stones to almost all of them. I'm not particularly devoted to any faith or religious dogma; but in this land, the gravitational pull of spirituality is immense. The forces of nature are so overwhelming and evident that mere survival can never be taken for granted. Life itself is full of hardships, and death visits often. Like no other country that I've visited, Mongolia has led me to understand the need to appeal to a higher power for peace of mind.

One particular force of nature has been a constant adversary of mine throughout my journey—the wind. Like a slap in the face, I was introduced to the wind early in the expedition when my tent bounded into the Kherlen River. That incident on hole one was an eye-opening lesson; but just in case I had grown complacent about the wind's dominion over this rugged landscape, Mongolia served up a fierce reminder on hole eighteen.

Five days ago, I hit my way out of Zereg *sum* (county), a region that presented several challenging obstacles, including the most ferocious congregation of mosquitoes anywhere on Mongolia's steppe, and a terrain consisting of waist-high reeds in the valley floor and scrabble-covered barren slopes at the base of the hills. As the prevalence of satisfactory golfing grass diminished, I was forced to hit amongst the rocks, using dried animal dung or pieces of shrubbery as tees. My days in this county were filled with mosquito-slapping frustration, and my nights were spent with my tent pitched among sharp rocks and concretionary soils. My final night brought an unwelcome visitor.

It was a calm evening when I climbed into my tent under a burning orange 10:00 P.M. sunset; but after a couple hours, the wind started to pick up. I woke in the night with my tent wildly shaking and flapping, and I began to worry that this could be the onset of one of those legendary Gobi dust storms that I've read about. As the wind continued to grow in intensity, I rolled onto the upwind side of the tent to help anchor it. But by this time, sand and dust were whipping around inside the tent, blasting around the rain fly and through the mesh lining of the inner wall. I covered my face and hunkered down, naively thinking I could endure the storm. But the wind blew harder still.

Sierra Designs claims that this tent can withstand a 60 mph (100 km/h) wind. I didn't need a meteorologist with an anemometer to realize that this wind would seriously test that claim. Not wanting to release my weight from the upwind edge of the tent floor, I dragged my backpack up with my feet to provide an additional anchor.

Khatanbaatar's instincts, or the rocking of his jeep in the gale, had woken him and aroused his sense of impending disaster. I was pleased to hear the engine in his jeep roar and pull up within a few feet of my tent in an effort to block some of the wind. But it was too little, too late. I could feel my body being lifted off the earth by the force of the wind stretching the tent fabric like a sail. One of the stakes pulled up, a pole snapped, and the tent began to cave in on itself, signaling the end of its structural integrity and any hope that I could have weathered the storm.

I yelled to Khatanbaatar for help. He bravely left the security of his jeep and stood on top of the tent as I struggled to find the zipper in the flailing fabric and blinding dust. As I opened the flap, articles began to fly off like bullets into the darkness—my sleeping bag stuff sack, a map, a pair of socks. Once outside, the fury of the noc-turnal maelstrom intensified, and Khatanbaatar and I screamed instructions to each other in the pitch-black night while shielding our faces from the stinging sand and dust. Miraculously, we held on to the tent and stuffed it inside the jeep as aluminum poles buckled and articles from my backpack spilled onto the floor. Emotionally shaken, I restlessly passed the night in the front seat of the swaying jeep, contemplating the vulnerability of a man in a tent in the vio-lent wrath of a Mongolian storm.

Khatanbaatar, in a calm display of Mongolian ingenuity, would repair my tent the following morning with a hodgepodge collection of nuts and bolts from his toolbox. Had I been alone, the destruction of my tent and probable physical harm to my health would have catastrophically altered the fate of my expedition. So near the end of my long journey, it disturbed me to consider such circumstances. Despite all my eagerness and dogged determination over the course of many months, my fate could have easily changed in one night.

It takes six more shots to reach Khatanbaatar and the ovoo at the top of the hill. A large stone monument in front of the rock pile welcomes travelers to the city of Khovd. Khatanbaatar sees my wide smile and reciprocates while pointing toward the valley ahead of us and the sprawled neighborhoods of gers and wooden houses that make up the city of Khovd. I walk to the eight-foot-high monolith and touch it lightly with my open hands as if to verify its existence. The stone monument is surprisingly cool in the heat of the midday sun and, despite its hardness, it's comforting to the touch. I walk a few more steps to the ovoo and make three circum-ambulations in a clockwise direction around its ten-foot diameter. Then I reach into my pocket and retrieve a golf ball. I place it thoughtfully on the pile of stones and look up to the heavens.

Golfers have for centuries waxed philosophical about the gods of golf: the benevolent deities who direct the ball into the cup for a hole-in-one, and the angry gods who steer the tee shot into the water hazard. Many believe that the gods of golf are variants of the pagan spirits who were worshipped centuries ago in Scotland where the game was invented. I'm not sure of their origin or form; but, as one who has spent many Sundays walking the links, I'm inclined to believe in their existence.

Standing now at this ovoo, the pull of spirituality is irresistible. I've golfed more than two thousand kilometers across an entire country. My health is intact, my three-iron is battered but unbroken, and I've accomplished the most challenging task that I've ever created for myself—one that will likely stand unparalleled in my life. I don't know if I have the Mongolian sky spirit, Tenger, to thank for this or the Highland gods of golf, but I do feel compelled to leave an offering, and a golf ball seems most appropriate.

Almost exactly two years ago, I discussed the idea of the expedition with my brother, Paul, while we were camping in the mountains of Colorado. We mulled over several public-relations strategies until an idea struck me. "I'll do it to raise awareness," I said. I imagined the journalists looking up from their notebooks and asking me: "Awareness of what?"

"Just awareness in general," I would answer. "There are far too many people in the world who are far too unaware."

The concept seemed to perfectly capture the absurdity of one man hitting a golf ball across Mongolia. I didn't need a cause or a reason to embark on this journey. I chose it because it was there. The public could interpret it in whatever way they wanted: a sporting challenge, an artistic expression, a new vision for the sport of golf, or an educational exploration of a unique land. None of these aspects was more important to me than any other. I just knew that I had to do it.

But during this journey, I've learned that "awareness" as an

existential concept just may exist. It has to do with one's understanding of his or her place in the world. The unique sequence of
events that puts you in one particular place at one particular time, a
four-dimensional conflagration of time and space. It's an understanding of the interconnectivity of natural forces, which are beyond
our control, and human relations, which are self-determined by a
collective human consciousness. Manifestations of "awareness" are
social responsibility and a humble, questioning inner voice. Ignorance, war, and intolerance are demonstrations of its absence.

My caddy, Khatanbaatar, continues to tell people we meet that
I'm playing baseball across Mongolia, despite my numerous
attempts at correcting him. I, on the other hand, continually miss
the sightings of antelope, rabbits, and other wildlife that he tries to
point out to me in the Mongolian landscape. We both laughed
when we saw a group of gers that was set up by Chinese construction workers who were building a section of the Millennium Road.
According to tradition, every ger in Mongolia is erected with the
door facing south. Even *I* know that. But these gers were facing
north, east, and west without any respect for the local customs. In
varying degrees, all of these examples point, quite simply, to a lack
of awareness.

I recently overheard a tourist describe the Mongolian countryside as "a good place to get some thinking done." As pure unadul-
terated nature, it has the ability to remove us from the complex
structures of human habitation and what we call "civilization." But

unlike the raw nature of a dense forest, Mongolia's open steppe is exposed in front of our eyes. It has no secrets. This overt display of the physical world has the dual ability to inspire and to comfort. It's no accident that meditative philosophies such as Buddhism have thrived in places like Mongolia and Tibet, which feature vast, wide-open landscapes.

Although golf and the associated counting of my steps and golf shots throughout each day have served as my primary means of meditation, I've spent countless hours sitting in the Mongolian steppe on terrain that has no name. Aside from the artificial GPS coordinates that I assign to my locations, the exact spot of my ass on the ground has no significance. Nomadic Mongolian herders, like Native Americans and many indigenous cultures, have never placed a great importance on political boundaries. In these societies, land has always been considered communal, and in many cases the earth has been viewed as an entity outside the human realm.

Sitting alone and watching the shadows of clouds dance across the sun-drenched fields and climb effortlessly up the parabolic slopes of rugged mountains, I've gained a greater understanding of nature. Millions of years of geologic and biologic processes are on display as I view the bare craggy mountain peaks, the sparsely veg-etated foothills below them, and then the fertile valley floors where beetles roll balls of dried dung amongst fresh sprouts of grass. These processes began long before human evolution and will continue long after our species has disappeared. With considerable

opportunity to view and ponder these phenomena, I've come to recognize that the significance of my own existence is less relevant. In
short, I've become more aware.

I doubt that my expedition will have the impact I had hoped on
raising the collective awareness of the world, but I was pleased to
learn of an event that took place in the small town where I grew up
in New Hampshire. A reporter from the local newspaper had
written a story about me, and a couple months later she called my
parents. She simply wanted to tell them that she had just heard a
news story about Mongolia and Mongolian cuisine on National
Public Radio. Small talk and friendly conversations are not
uncommon in a small town, but having Mongolia as a catalyst for
them certainly is. Because of this expedition, she—and, I hope,
many others—will take a greater interest in this country. Mongolia
is a unique and beautiful land whose people share a rich culture and
a fascinating history. It deserves to have its place in the world.

With the attainment of a long-sought goal within my grasp, I
leave philosophical musings for another day and return to the business at hand. I have three more kilometers to golf. I tee the ball up
on a tuft of grass to the left of the ovoo and swing away. With a
steep downward slope in front of me, the ball flies, bounces, and
then rolls hundreds of yards for what may be my longest shot of the
expedition. Amidst a nagging swarm of mosquitoes, I chase down
the ball and continue swinging away until the road turns to asphalt
and a small wooden shack and a lowered gate across the road mark

the entrance to the city. The local police stop each vehicle that passes
through this gateway to the city, and Khatanbaatar has already con-
versed with them and possibly paid a small toll by the time I pick
up the 510th golf ball that I've used to cross the country and walk
toward his jeep.

Khovd is hardly distinguishable from any other Mongolian city,
but its special significance for me is incomparable. This city represents a Shangri-La, a sanctuary of conclusion to my restless journey.
Khovd has only been a dream for me until now. But, as Khatanbaatar and I discuss mundane things like which hotel to choose and
where to eat, I worry that the end of my expedition will be under-
whelmingly anticlimactic. I want to run through the streets
screaming, "I did it! I did it!" and receive applause and accolades
from the city's mayor. But I'm unlikely to find the response I crave
from the local residents; and to make matters worse, by the time I
reach the central post office, it's closed. This is the only place in a
two-hundred-mile radius where it's possible to make an international phone call, and I've just learned that it'll be closed for the
next three days because of the Naadam holiday.

My enthusiasm curbed by my solitude as a foreigner in a foreign
land, I walk through the streets of Khovd until, quite serendipi-
tously, I bump into Barry, an American wildlife biologist. Barry's
been up in the mountains counting and documenting Argali sheep
droppings, so I get the impression that he'll be a willing audience to
the enthusiastic ramblings of my adventure. We settle into a table in

the empty restaurant attached to my hotel and purchase two bottles of beer from the adjacent convenience store. Halfway through my dissertation on the advantages of using a three-iron for cross-country golf, I hear a familiar voice call my name.

Daniel, whom I had met while traveling in Mongolia in 2001, is standing behind me with an enormous grin on his face. "I can't believe you actually made it," he exclaims between laughs. "And I can't believe how easily we found you."

I stand and give my friend a hug. "Well, there are only three hotels in town," I reply. "You had pretty good odds."

Daniel and I had become friends after our chance meeting three years ago, and he was extremely supportive of my expedition plan. So supportive, in fact, that when he decided to travel for a couple months between jobs this year, he penciled in Khovd for early July.

Daniel takes a seat at the table along with his girlfriend, Rachel, and their traveling companion, Jon, an American who lives in Hong Kong. The three of them plan to spend a month in Western Mongolia.

"André sent me an e-mail a few weeks ago that said 'I'll see you in Khovd on July tenth,'" Daniel explains to Barry. "And here he is. This is incredible."

It seems fitting that Daniel is here at the conclusion of my journey. He was with me at its genesis on September 11, 2001, on a cool evening where we sipped vodka in the Mongolian countryside, enjoying the splendors of our surroundings, oblivious to world events. When I mentioned the original idea to him back then, he gave me a look that said, "You're absolutely crazy"; but I got the impression that he was quite confident that I'd actually attempt it.

"So, how do you feel?" he asks.

I take a sip from the tall brown bottle of Borigo beer that I clutch in my right hand. I fidget with the corner of the blue-and-white label with my left hand as I look up at Daniel.

"I'm tired."

It's the most honest answer that I can give. Physically, mentally, and emotionally, I'm exhausted. If I were asked to do it all over again, I'd either collapse into a catatonic heap of misery or I'd jump from a bridge. I couldn't possibly spend another minute scanning the grass for a tiny white ball and, provided that I found it, continue hitting it toward an invisible target. It was an exercise that is best done once, and only once.

This was a test of personal endurance that I created for myself. One which, although challenging, strung together two of my greatest interests, travel and golf. As I sit now with friends around me and a cold beer in my hand, I can bask in the satisfaction of knowing that I passed my self-created endurance test. I golfed across Mongolia.

As a young boy playing golf on a small nine-hole course in New Hampshire, I used to fantasize about sinking the winning putt on the eighteenth hole at Augusta National Country Club, site of the Masters golf tournament. Winning the Masters is the pinnacle of golf achievement, and every young golfer dreams of one day having a shot at its undulating fairways and greens surrounded by majestic pines and flowering azaleas, vying for the championship with the world's greatest golfers. The reality for me now, at the age of thirty-five, is that I'll never be better than a fifteen-handicap golfer. My talent has its limits. I'll never be able to add my name to the list of golf's greatest players who have triumphed at Augusta: Arnold Palmer, Jack Nicklaus, Tiger Woods. But at this moment, I am certain of another fact. The list of golfers who have golfed across Mongolia is a very short list. As of now, that list has only one name.

AUG   2006